THE GOSPEL OF

JOHN

PART 1
CHAPTERS 1–8

WILLIAM MACDONALD

Developed as a study course by Emmaus Correspondence School, founded in 1942.

ECS Ministries exists to glorify God by providing biblically-sound resources and structured study materials for the purpose of teaching people from every nation to know Jesus Christ as Savior and to live in a way that is consistent with God's Word.

The Gospel of John — Part 1
William MacDonald

Published by:
Emmaus Correspondence School
(A division of ECS Ministries)
PO Box 1028
Dubuque, IA 52004-1028
phone: (563) 585-2070
email: orders@emmauscourses.org
website: www.emmauscourses.org

First Edition 2017 (AK '17), 2 UNITS
ISBN 978-1-59387-148-2
Code: JOHN1

Course Copyright © 2017 ECS Ministries
Text Copyright © 1962, 2017 William MacDonald

Many Bible study courses may also be taken via smart phones, tablets, and computers. For more information, visit: www.emmauscourses.org

Previously published as part of *The Gospel of John*, copyright © 1962, 1972, 2004, 2006 by William MacDonald. Published by ECS Ministries.

All rights in this course are reserved. No part of this publication may be reproduced or transmitted in any manner, electronic or mechanical, including photocopy, recording, or any information storage and retrieval system including the Internet without written permission from the publisher. Permission is not needed for brief quotations embodied in critical articles and reviews.

All Scripture quotations, unless otherwise indicated, are taken from the New King James Version. Copyright © 1979, 1980, 1982 by Thomas Nelson, Inc. Used by permission. All rights reserved.

Printed in the United States of America

COURSE OVERVIEW

John the apostle wrote his gospel many years after Matthew, Mark, and Luke had penned theirs. Already the church was being plagued by error and attacks upon the person and work of God's beloved Son, so under the inspiration of the Holy Spirit, John sought to give clear testimony to the deity of Jesus Christ. He concentrates on presenting the miracles and words of Jesus and then interpreting them for his readers. His goal? That you, the reader, ". . . may believe that Jesus is the Christ, the Son of God, and that believing you may have life in His name" (John 20:31).

This course covers the first 8 chapters of John's gospel.

LESSONS YOU WILL STUDY

1. Jesus Christ Is God Incarnate (John 1:1-18) 5
2. John the Baptist Fulfills His Mission (John 1:19-51) 15
3. Jesus Begins His Public Ministry (John 2) 21
4. Jesus and John the Baptist Reveal the Way into the Kingdom (John 3) 27
5. Jesus Reveals Himself to the Samaritans (John 4:1-42) 37
6. Jesus Ministers to Individuals in Galilee and Jerusalem (John 4:43–5:23) 47
7. Jesus Defends His God-Given Authority (John 5:24-47) 55
8. Jesus Feeds 5000+ and Teaches about the Bread from Heaven (John 6:1-34) 63
9. Jesus Is the Bread of Life (John 6:35-59) 69
10. Jesus' Teaching Creates Controversy (John 6:60–7:24) 75
11. Jesus Is the Light of the World (John 7:25–8:20) 81
12. Jesus Debates with the Pharisees (John 8:21-59) 89

STUDENT INSTRUCTIONS

How to Study

This course has two parts—the lesson content and the exam booklet. Before you begin to study, ask God to open your heart so that you can receive the truths that He wants to teach you from His Word. The study of the Bible brings great discoveries and bears rich fruit in the life of a believer. The following study guidelines will be helpful in order to gain the most from this course.

Read each chapter through at least twice, once to get a general idea of its content and then again, slowly, looking up any Bible references given. It is important that you read the Bible passages referenced as some questions may be based on the Bible text. We suggest that you keep a regular schedule by trying to complete at least one chapter per week.

Exams

At the end of the course there is an exam booklet with one exam for each lesson. (If a Single Page Answer Sheet is also included, **carefully read all instructions** and completely fill it out before mailing it in for grading.) Do not answer the questions by what you think or have always believed. The questions are designed to find out if you understand the material in the course.

At the end of each exam, there is a *What Do You Say?* question. These questions are included for your own reflection. They will not be counted as part of your grade, but instead provide an opportunity for you to personally meditate on the lesson.

Getting Exams Graded

When you have answered all the exam questions, fill in your contact information and mail it back to the instructor, associated ministry, or organization from which you received it. After finishing this course with a passing average, you will be awarded a certificate.

We are excited to be a part of your study of God's Word. May the Lord bless your study of His Word with joy and fruitfulness!

CHAPTER

1

JESUS CHRIST IS GOD INCARNATE
JOHN 1:1-18

Introduction to the Book

Charles R. Erdman wrote of John's gospel, "It has induced more persons to follow Christ, it has inspired more believers to loyal service, it has presented to scholars more difficult problems than any other book that could be named."

The apostle John expressed his purpose for writing his account of the life of Jesus Christ near the end of the book, in chapter 20 verse 31. Acknowledging the fact that Jesus had performed many miracles that he did not include in his book, John wrote:

> "But *these* are written that you may believe that Jesus is the Christ, the Son of God, and that believing you may have life in His name."

The seven public miracles—*signs*—that John did include "point" the reader to the fact that Jesus is God and the One sent by God; He was God's designated Messiah, the Anointed ("Chosen") One. Those miracles were

> The seven public miracles "point" the reader to the fact that Jesus is God and the One sent by God.

1. Turning water into wine at the wedding in Cana of Galilee (2:9)
2. Healing the nobleman's son (4:46-54)
3. Healing the crippled man at the pool of Bethesda (5:2-9)
4. Feeding the five thousand (6:1-14)

5. Walking on the Sea of Galilee, calming the wind, and bringing the boat immediately to its destination (6:16-21)
6. Healing the man who was blind from birth (9:1-7)
7. Raising Lazarus from the dead (11:1-44)

In addition to these, John recorded an eighth sign-miracle, a post-resurrection one, which only His disciples witnessed: the miraculous catch of fish (21:1-14).

The *authorship* of this gospel has been greatly debated. This is undoubtedly because it gives such clear testimony to the deity of Jesus Christ. The attack has sought to prove that the account was not the work of an eyewitness but of an unknown genius who lived 50 to 100 years later. Thus it is supposed to reflect the church's thinking about Christ and does not comprise a record of what He Himself actually was, said, or did.

The gospel itself is anonymous as to authorship, but there are many good reasons for believing it was written by John the apostle, one of Christ's twelve disciples. For example, the author was a Jew—the style of writing, the vocabulary, the familiarity with Jewish customs and characteristics, and the background of the Old Testament reflected in this gospel all speak strongly of this. He was a Jew who lived in Palestine (1:28; 2:1, 11; 4:46; 11:18, 54; 21:1-2). He knew Jerusalem and the temple intimately (5:2; 9:7; 18:1; 19:13, 17, 20, 41; also see 2:14-16; 8:20; 10:22). He was an eyewitness of what he narrates—details of places, persons, time, manner, etc. (4:46; 5:14; 6:59; 12:21; 13:1; 14:5, 8; 18:6; 19:31). He shows intimate knowledge of the inner circle of the disciples and of Christ Himself (6:19, 60-61; 12:16; 13:22, 28; 16:19). Since the author is precise in naming other disciples yet does not name himself, it is presumed that the unnamed person of 13:23; 19:26; 20:2; 21:7, 20 is the apostle John. Three important verses for further consideration of the eyewitness character of the author are 1:14, 19:35, and 21:24.

The *chronology* of our Lord's earthly ministry is gained from this gospel. From the other three gospels, Christ's ministry would appear to have lasted only one year. The references to the annual feasts in John supply us with the duration of approximately three years for His public ministry. Note these references: a first Feast of Passover (2:12-13); "a feast" (5:1), possibly Passover or Purim; a second Feast of Passover (6:4); the Feast of Tabernacles (7:2); the Feast of Dedication (10:22); and the last (third) Feast of Passover (12:1). John is also precise in his references to time. While the other three writers are generally content with approximate references, such as the third or ninth hours, John mentions the seventh hour (4:52), the third day (2:1), two days (11:6), and six days (12:1).

The *style and vocabulary* of this gospel are unique except for the epistles of John. The sentences are short and simple. Usually, the shorter the sentence is, the weightier the truth. The vocabulary is the most limited of all the gospels, yet the most profound in meaning. Author Leon Morris observed it is like a pool in which a child can wade and in which an elephant can swim. Note these important words and the number of their occurrences: Father (118), believe (100), world (78), love (45), life (37), witness, bear record, etc. (47), light (24), etc.

> In this gospel, the Spirit of God perfects and completes the revelation of God in the person of Jesus Christ.

One marked feature of this gospel is the occurrence of the number seven and its multiples. The ideas of perfection and completion attach to this number throughout Scripture (see Genesis 2:1-3). In this gospel, the Spirit of God perfects and completes the revelation of God in the person of Jesus Christ, so patterns based on the number seven are frequent.

The record of Jesus saying "I am . . ." many times is a feature of this gospel. These are the bread of life (6:35, 41, 48, 51); the light of the world (8:12; 9:5); the door (10:7, 9); the good shepherd (10:11, 14); the resurrection and the life (11:25); the way, the truth, and the life (14:6); and the true vine (15:1, 5). Not so familiar are the seven occurrences of "I am" without a predicate (that is, the simple statement). These are found in 4:26; 6:20; 8:24, 28, 58; 13:19; and 18:5, 8. The last one is a double one.

The Purpose of the Prologue

John 1:1-18 is commonly described as a *prologue* because it introduces John's subject in the same way that a prologue to a play primes an audience for the upcoming characters and action. In his prologue, John proclaims several facets of the person and work of Jesus Christ which he goes on to give evidence of in the following chapters.

John begins his gospel by speaking about *the Word*—but he does not explain at first who or what the Word is. We may define the term *word* as "a unit of speech by which we express ourselves to others." But John is not speaking about a unit of speech; he is speaking about a person—the Lord Jesus Christ, the Son of God. John speaks of Him as "the Word" because God has fully expressed Himself to mankind in the person of the Lord Jesus. The Son of God came into the world to reveal to mankind what God is like. And by dying for us on the cross of Calvary, He revealed how much God loves mankind. Thus Christ is God's living Word to man, the expression of God's thoughts.

> By dying for us on the cross of Calvary, Jesus revealed how much God loves mankind.

"The Word was God" (vv. 1-5)

John opens in verse 1 with a statement that Christ existed from all eternity. As far as the human mind can go back, Christ was there. He never was created. He had no beginning. "The Word was with God." He had a separate and distinct personality. He was a real person who lived with God. He not only dwelt *with* God, but *was* God. The Bible teaches there is one God and that there are three persons in the Godhead—the Father, the Son, and the Holy Spirit. All three of these persons are God. In this verse, two of the persons of the Godhead are mentioned: the Father and the Son. It is the first of many clear statements in this gospel that *Jesus Christ is God.* It is not enough to say that He is a god, that He is godlike, or even that He is divine. The Bible teaches that He *is God.*

Verse 2 appears to be a repetition of what has already been said, but actually it is not. This verse teaches that Christ's personality and deity were without beginning. He did not become a person for the first time when He was born. Nor did He somehow become a god after His resurrection. He is God from all eternity.

He Himself was not a created being; rather, He was the Creator of all things—mankind, the animals, the heavenly planets, the angels—all things visible and invisible. If a thing was made, He made it. As Creator, He is, of course, superior to anything He has created. Actually, according to Scripture, all three persons of the Godhead were involved in the work of creation: "God created the heavens and the earth" (Gen. 1:1). "The Spirit of God was hovering over the face of the waters" (Gen. 1:2). "All things were created through Him [Christ] and for Him" (Col. 1:16).

He was (and is) the source of life. The word here in verse 4 includes both physical and spiritual life. When we were born, we received physical life. When we are born again, we receive spiritual life. Both come from Him. He is also the light of men. He provides the guidance and direction we need. It is one thing to exist, but another to know how to live—to know the true purpose of life and the way to heaven. The same One who gave us life is the One who provides us with light for the path we travel in life.

> **The same One who gave us life is the One who provides us with light for the path we travel in life.**

Notice the seven wonderful titles of our Lord Jesus Christ in this opening chapter. He is called the Word (vv. 1, 14); the Light (vv. 5, 7); the Lamb of God (vv. 29, 36); the Son of God (vv. 34, 49); the Christ (Messiah) (v. 41); the King of Israel (v. 49); and the Son of Man (v. 51). The first four titles seem to be universal in application. The last three titles had their first application to Israel, God's ancient people.

The entrance of sin brought darkness to the minds of human beings (v. 5). It plunged the world into darkness in the sense that people in general neither knew God nor wanted to. Into this darkness stepped the Lord Jesus—a light shining in a dark place. "The darkness did not comprehend it," we read. This may mean that the darkness did not understand the Lord Jesus when He came into the world. People did not realize who He really was or why He had come. Another interpretation is conveyed in other Bible versions: ". . . the darkness did not overcome it." Here the thought is that man's rejection and enmity did not prevent the true light from shining.

"There was a man . . . whose name was John" (vv. 6-8)

These verses refer to John the Baptist, who was sent by God as a forerunner of the Lord Jesus. His mission was to announce the coming of Christ and to tell the Jews to get ready to receive Him. He came to testify to the fact that Jesus was truly the Light of the world and thus worthy of their worship, allegiance, and trust. John did not attract attention to himself, for then he would have been unfaithful to his appointed task. He pointed people to Jesus and not to himself.

"Grace and truth came through Jesus Christ" (vv. 9-18)

Jesus Is the Light

Other persons down through the ages have claimed to be guides and saviors, but the One to whom John witnessed was the genuine Light, the best and the truest Light (v. 9). Another translation of this verse is, "The true Light, which, coming into the world, gives light to every man." In other words, the expression "coming into the world" describes "the true Light," not "every man." This does not mean that every person has received some inward knowledge concerning Christ. Neither does it mean that everyone has heard about the Lord Jesus at one time or another. It means that the Light shines upon all people everywhere, revealing their true character. By His coming into the world as the perfect Man, He has shown how imperfect all other human beings are. When a room is in darkness, you do not see the dust on the furniture. But when the light is switched on, the room is seen as it actually is. In that same sense, the shining of the true Light reveals man as he actually is.

Jesus Is the Creator

From the time of His birth in Bethlehem until the day He went back to heaven, Jesus Christ lived in this world (v. 10). Indeed, He had more right to be here than anyone else. He had brought the whole world into being and was its rightful Owner. Instead of recognizing Him as the Creator, most people thought He was just another man like them. As a result, they treated Him like a stranger and an outcast and rejected Him.

Jesus Is the Savior

"He came to His own [things]," we read in verse 11. He was not trespassing on someone else's property. He was actually living on a planet He Himself had made! Moreover, "His own [people] did not receive Him." In a general sense, this might refer to all mankind, and it is true that He was almost universally rejected. But in a special sense, the Jewish nation was

His own;" they were His chosen, earthly people. When He came into the world, He presented Himself to the Jews as their Messiah, but they would not receive Him. Now He offers Himself to all mankind again, and to those who receive Him He gives the right, the authority, to become children of God (v. 12). This verse tells us clearly how we can become children of God. It is not by good works, not by church membership, not by doing one's best, but by receiving Him, by believing in "His name"—comprehensively embracing His person and His work.

To become a child in a physical sense, one must be born. So to become a child of God, one must have a second birth. This is known as *the new birth* or *conversion*. Verse 13 gives us three ways by which the new birth does *not* take place, and the one way by which it *does*. First, it is "not of blood." This means that a person does not become a Christian through having Christian parents; salvation is not passed down from parent to child through the blood stream. Neither is it "of the will of the flesh." In other words, a person does not have the power in his own flesh or will to produce the new birth. Nor is new birth accomplished "of the will of man." No human being can save another human being. A preacher, for instance, may be very anxious to see a certain person born again, but he does not have the power to produce this marvelous birth. How, then, does this birth take place? The answer is found in the words "but of God." This means simply that the power to produce the new birth does not rest with anything or anyone but God.

> We can become children of God by receiving Christ, by embracing His person and His work.

Jesus Is the Incarnate One

The "Word became flesh" when Jesus was born as a baby in Bethlehem (v. 14). He had always existed as the Son of God with the Father in heaven, but He now came into the world in a human body. He was never made or created; He Himself was the Creator of all things. But He became flesh in the sense that He came into the world as a man.

He "dwelt among us," we read. It was not just a short appearance, about which there might be some mistake or misunderstanding. God actually came to this earth and lived here as a man among men. The word "dwelt" means "tabernacled" or "pitched His tent." His body was the tent in which He dwelt among human beings for thirty-three years.

"And we beheld His glory," says John. In the Bible, *glory* is the word often used to convey the bright, shining light which was seen when God was present. It also means the perfection and excellence of God. When the Lord Jesus was here on earth, He veiled (covered) His glory in a body of flesh. There were two ways in which His glory did become manifest, however. First, there was His moral glory—the radiance of His perfect life and character. There was no flaw or blemish in Him. He was perfect in all His ways, and it showed. Every virtue was manifested in His life in exquisite balance. Second, there was the visible outshining of His glory which took place on the Mount of Transfiguration (Matt. 17:1-2). The glory the disciples saw confirmed to them that He was truly the Son of God. Jesus is "the only begotten of the Father," that is, He is God's unique Son. God did not have any other Son like Him. In one sense, all true believers are sons of God. But Jesus is the Son of God in a class all by Himself. As the Son of God, He is equal with God.

John describes Jesus as "full of grace and truth." He treated people with kindness they did not deserve. But He was also completely honest and upright, and He never excused sin or approved evil. To be completely gracious and at the same time completely righteous is something only God can be.

> To be completely gracious and at the same time completely righteous is something only God can be.

Jesus Is the Son of God

We read in verse 15 that John the Baptist testified to Jesus being the Son of God. Before Jesus entered upon His public ministry, John had been telling people about Him. When Jesus did arrive upon the scene, John said, in effect, "This is the One I have been describing to you." Jesus came "*after*" John so far as His birth and ministry were concerned; He was born six months after John and presented Himself to the people of Israel some time after John had been preaching and baptizing. Yet Jesus was "preferred before" John. He was greater than John—worthy of more honor—for the simple reason that He had existed from all eternity as the Son of God.

All who put their faith in the Lord Jesus for the salvation of their souls receive spiritual strength out of His fullness (v. 16). His fullness is so great that He can provide for all Christians in all countries and in all ages. The expression "grace for grace" probably means "grace upon grace," or "abundant grace." Here "grace" means God's gracious favor, His kindness, which He showers upon His beloved children.

In verse 17 John contrasts the Old Testament period and the New Testament era. The Law given by Moses was not a display of grace. It commanded men and women to obey, and it condemned them if they failed to do so. It told them what was right but did not give them the power to do it. It was given to show them that they were sinners, but it could not save them from their sins. "But grace and truth came through Jesus Christ." He did not come to judge the world but to save those who were unworthy, who could not save themselves, and who were His enemies. That is grace—heaven's best for earth's worst.

> Christ came to save those who were unworthy, who could not save themselves. That is grace—heaven's best for earth's worst.

Not only did grace come through Jesus Christ, but truth came through Him as well. He said of Himself, "I am . . . the truth." He did not show grace at the expense of truth. Although He loved sinners, He did not love their sins.

"No man has seen God at any time," says John in verse 18. God is spirit and therefore is invisible. He does not have a human body. Although He did appear to people in the Old Testament in visible form as an angel or as a man, these appearances did not reveal what God is really like. They were merely temporary appearances by which He chose to communicate to His people. The Lord Jesus is God's only begotten Son; He is God's unique Son; there is no other Son like Him. He ever occupies a place of special nearness to God the Father. Even when He was here on earth, Jesus was still "in the bosom of the Father" in terms of relationship and oneness. He was one with God and equal with God. He has fully revealed to mankind what God is like. When people saw Jesus, they saw God. They heard God speak. They felt God's love and tenderness. God's thoughts and attitudes toward mankind have been fully told out by Christ.

CHAPTER

2

JOHN THE BAPTIST FULFILLS HIS MISSION
JOHN 1:19-51

"Behold! The Lamb of God" (vv. 19-34)

When news reached Jerusalem that a man named John was telling the nation to repent because the Messiah was coming, the Jews sent a committee of priests and Levites to find out who this man was. Priests were those who carried on important rituals in the temple, while Levites were servants who attended to the practical duties there. "Who are you?" they asked. "Are you the long-awaited Messiah?"

Other men might have seized this opportunity for fame by claiming to be the Messiah. But John was a true and faithful witness. He testified that he was not the Christ, that is, the Messiah (*Christ* is the transliteration of the Greek word *Christos,* which equates to the Hebrew term *Messiah,* meaning "anointed, chosen one"). The Jews expected the prophet Elijah to return to the earth prior to Messiah's coming (Mal. 4:5). So they reasoned that if John was not the Messiah, then perhaps he was Elijah. But John assured them he was not (v. 21). In Deuteronomy 18:15, Moses had said, "The LORD your God will raise up for you a Prophet like me from your midst, from your brethren. Him you shall hear." The Jews remembered this prediction and thought that John might be the prophet mentioned by Moses. But again John said that it was not so.

The delegation would have been embarrassed to return to Jerusalem without a definite answer, and so they pressed John. He responded, "I am the voice of one crying in the wilderness," quoting from Isaiah 40:3. In other words, John was the predicted "forerunner": he was the voice, and Israel was the wilderness. The Israelites had become dry and barren, like a desert. John spoke of himself simply as a voice—a voice not to be seen, only heard. John was the voice, but Christ was the Word. A word needs a voice to make it known, and a voice is of no value without a word to speak. The Word is infinitely greater than the voice. It is our privilege, too, to be a voice for Christ.

> John was the voice, but Christ was the Word. It is our privilege, too, to be a voice for Christ.

John's message was, "Make straight the way of the LORD." In other words, "The Messiah is coming. Remove everything in your life that would keep you from receiving Him. Repent of your sins so you will be in the right spirit to accept His right to rule over you as your King."

The Pharisees who made up the delegation were a strict sect of the Jews who prided themselves on their superior knowledge of the Law and on their efforts to carry out not only its most minute instructions, but many that had been added in the intertestamental period. Actually, many of the Pharisees were hypocrites; they appeared to be religious, but their lives and lifestyles did not reflect the godliness that should have characterized them. They demanded to know what authority John had for baptizing people. John did not want anyone to think that *he* was important. His task was simply to prepare Israel for their coming King. Whenever his hearers repented of their sins, he baptized them in water as an outward symbol of their inward change of heart.

"Do not think of me as a great man," said John in effect. "I'm not even worthy enough to untie the sandal straps of the One I am heralding and who is in your midst even now." John's humility and his intent to honor the Messiah he proclaimed is very evident.

The next day, John saw Jesus approaching him (v. 29). In the thrill of that moment, he cried out, "Behold! The Lamb of God who takes away the sin of the world!" The lamb was a sacrificial animal to Jews. God had instructed them to slay a lamb and sprinkle its blood on the altar as a sacrifice. The lamb was killed as a substitute so that the sins of the offerer might be covered, forgiven. However, the blood of all the lambs shed during the Old Testament period did not really put away sin. Those lambs were pictures—types—pointing forward to the Lamb whom God would Himself provide to actually *carry (bear) away* sins, not just cover them. For several hundred years, godly Jews had waited for the coming of this Lamb. Now at last He was here, and John the Baptist triumphantly announced His arrival—the true Lamb of God.

When John said that Jesus bears the sin of "the world," he did not mean that the sins committed by *all* people are thereby forgiven. It is true to say that the death of the Lord Jesus was great enough in value to pay for the sins of the whole world, but only those who receive Him as Lord and Savior are forgiven the sins they commit personally.

John never grew weary of reminding people that he was only preparing the way for Someone greater than himself (v. 30). Jesus was greater than John to the same extent that God is greater than man. When John said, "I did not know Him" (v. 31), he did not mean that he had never seen Him before. John and Jesus were cousins, so almost certainly knew each other. But John had not recognized his cousin as being the Messiah, and did not do so until the time of His baptism. John's mission was to point the Messiah out to the people of Israel when He appeared. He baptized people in water to mark their decision to prepare themselves for Christ's coming, not to attract followers to himself.

> **John never grew weary of reminding people that he was only preparing the way for Someone greater than himself.**

John baptized Jesus in the Jordan. After Jesus went up out of the water, the Spirit of God descended like a dove and rested on Him (Matt. 3:16). God had revealed to John that when the Messiah came, the Spirit of God would descend upon Him and stay on Him. Therefore, when this happened to Jesus, John realized that this was the One who would baptize with the Holy Spirit (v. 33). The Holy Spirit is one of the three persons in the Godhead. He is equal with God the Father and God the Son. The baptism with the Holy Spirit took place on the day of Pentecost (Acts 1:5 and Acts 2:4, 38) when the Spirit came down from heaven to dwell in the body of every believer and to make each believer a member of the church, the body of Christ (1 Cor. 12:13).

John now bore witness to the fact that Jesus of Nazareth was the Son of God who was foretold as coming into the world (v. 34).

"We have found the Messiah" (vv. 35-42)

The day mentioned here in verse 35 is the third specific day that has been mentioned. John the Baptist was with two of his own disciples (followers, learners). These men had heard John preach and believed what he said, but they had not yet met the Messiah he proclaimed was coming. Now John again bore public witness to Jesus being the Christ. He simply drew attention to His person. And by his faithful preaching, John lost two disciples but rejoiced to see them following Jesus.

The Savior is always interested in those who follow Him (v. 38). Here He showed His interest by turning to the two men and asking them, "What do you seek?" He wanted them to express their desire in their own words. Their answer showed they wanted to be with Him and to get to know Him better. They called Him "Rabbi," the Hebrew word for master, or teacher.

No one with a genuine desire to learn more of Jesus Christ is ever turned away. Jesus invited these two to His lodging. His invitation was extended to them about "the tenth hour" (i.e. 4 pm). One of these disciples was Andrew. The name of the other is not given to us, but Bible scholars assume it was John—the author of this gospel. They reason that humility kept him from mentioning his own name.

It is a biblical principle that whenever a person finds Jesus, he usually wants his relatives to meet Him too (v. 41). So Andrew went quickly to his brother Simon with the thrilling news: "We have found the Messiah." What an astounding announcement this was! For at least four thousand years, God's people had waited for the promised Christ, God's Anointed One. Now Simon hears from the lips of his own brother the startling news that the Messiah was nearby. Truly they were living when history was being made.

> We do not have to be great preachers or clever speakers; we need only to tell people about the Lord Jesus and what He did for us, and God will take care of the rest.

Andrew's message simply drew Simon to the Savior. There is a lesson here for us: We do not have to be great preachers or clever speakers; we need only to tell people about the Lord Jesus and what He did for us, and God will take care of the rest. Because of what Andrew did, Simon later became one of the leading apostles of Jesus Christ. Simon is better known than his brother, but Andrew will no doubt share his brother's reward, because it was Andrew who brought him to Jesus.

The Lord knew Simon's name without being told. He also knew that Simon had an unstable and timid character and that his character would be changed, that he would be as steady and firm as a stone—necessary traits for his leadership role in the early church. How did Jesus know all this? Because He was (and is) God. Simon's name did change to Cephas (same as Peter), and he became a man of strong character, especially after the ascension of the Lord and the descent of the Holy Spirit.

As a chronological side note, this incident predates Christ's *official* call of the four fishermen (Simon, Andrew, James, and John) that Mark records in Mark 1:16-20 and which took place some six months or more later.

"Rabbi, You are the Son of God" (vv. 43-51)

This was now the fourth day we have read about in this chapter. Jesus walked northward into the region known as Galilee. There it appears He sought out a man called Philip and invited him to be a follower. "Follow Me." These are great words—great because of the One who spoke them, and great because of the privilege they offered. Christ is still issuing this simple yet sublime invitation to all people everywhere.

Bethsaida was a city on the shores of the Sea of Galilee (v. 44), and Jesus performed some of His mighty miracles there (Luke 10:13). It was the home of Philip, Andrew, and Simon Peter. Yet it rejected Christ, and as a result it was destroyed so completely that we cannot tell now the exact spot where it was located.

Philip wanted to share his new-found joy with someone else, so he went and found Nathanael (v. 45). His message was simple and to the point. He told Nathanael that he had found the Messiah who had been foretold by Moses and the prophets—Jesus of Nazareth. Actually, his message was not entirely accurate in that he described Jesus as "the son of Joseph." Jesus was born of Mary when she was still a virgin, but He had no human father. Joseph adopted Jesus and thus became His legal father. J. S. Stewart says,

> "It never was Christ's way to demand a full-fledged faith for a beginning. It never was his way to hold men back from discipleship on the ground of an incomplete creed. And quite certainly that is not his way today. He puts himself alongside his brethren. He bids them attach themselves to him at any point they can. He takes them on with the faith that they can offer him. He is content with that as a beginning; and from that he leads his friends on, as he led the

first group on, step by step, to the inmost secret of who he is and to the full glory of discipleship."

Nathanael was not convinced, however. Nazareth was a despised city in Galilee, and it seemed impossible to him that the Messiah would live in a neighborhood of such ill-repute (v. 46). Philip did not argue with him. He realized that the best way to meet objections was to introduce him directly to Jesus—a valuable lesson for all who are seeking to win others to Christ. Don't argue. Don't engage in prolonged discussions. Just bid them to "come and see."

Verse 47 reveals to the reader a fact that testifies to Christ's omniscience (signifying His deity): without any previous acquaintance with Nathanael, Jesus declared him to be an Israelite in whom there was no trickery or deceit. The patriarch Jacob had a reputation for dishonesty, but Nathanael did not follow in his ancestor's footsteps. Nathanael was obviously surprised that a total stranger should speak to him as if He had known him previously. Apparently he had been completely concealed when he was sitting under the fig tree—but Jesus knew he was there. Perhaps it was the power of the Lord Jesus to see him when he was shut off from human view that convinced Nathanael. Or perhaps this knowledge was given to him in a supernatural way. In any event, he was now convinced that Jesus was the Son of God and the King of Israel.

The Lord had given Nathanael two proofs that He was the Messiah: He had described Nathanael's character, and He had seen Nathanael when no other eyes could have seen him. These two proofs were sufficient for Nathanael, and he believed (v. 50). But now Jesus stated that he would witness even greater proofs. John records Jesus introducing His statement with the words "Most assuredly." This is the first of several uses of the phrase in John's gospel, and conveys that Jesus was about to say something especially important. He gave Nathanael a glimpse into the future when He will come back to reign. In that day, the heavens will be opened. God's favor will rest upon the King as He reigns. The angels of God will ascend and descend upon Him. Angels are servants of God; they travel like flames of fire on His errands. When Jesus reigns as King, these angels will travel back and forth between heaven and earth, fulfilling His will.

Jesus was saying to Nathanael that what he had observed at this point in time comprised a minor demonstration of His messiahship compared to His full revelation as God's anointed Son. Then all mankind would know that something good *did* come out of Nazareth!

CHAPTER

3

JESUS BEGINS HIS PUBLIC MINISTRY
JOHN 2

"They have no wine" (vv. 1-11)

The "third day" mentioned in this verse no doubt refers to the third day of the Lord Jesus' stay in Galilee. In John 1:43 we read that Jesus went into Galilee. Cana is reckoned to have been near Capernaum and on higher ground.

There was a marriage in Cana on this particular day, and the mother of Jesus was in attendance. It is interesting to notice that Mary is spoken of as the mother of Jesus. The Lord Jesus was not famous because He was the son of the Virgin Mary; *she* was well-known because she was the mother of our Lord. The Scriptures always give the preeminent place to Christ and not to Mary (compare with several verses in Matthew 2, where the divine Author led the human author to always mention the Christ-child before Mary).

> Scriptures always give the preeminent place to Christ.

Jesus and His disciples (apparently just five in number at this point in time) were invited to the wedding (v. 2). When the mother of Jesus realized the hosts had run out of wine, she presented the problem to Jesus. She knew He had the power to solve the problem, and maybe she wanted Him to reveal Himself to the assembled guests as the Messiah. In the Scriptures, wine is often a picture of joy. When Mary said "They have no wine," she was unknowingly giving an accurate description of men and women who have never been saved. There is no real, lasting joy for the unbeliever.

The way Jesus replied (v. 4) seems to us to be very cold and distant. But it was not as strong a rebuke as it would seem. The word "woman" here is a title of respect, similar to the English word "lady." When Jesus asked, "What does your concern have to do with Me?" He was conveying that in performing His divine mission, He was not subject to instructions from her. Rather, He acted entirely in obedience to the will of God.

Mary had wanted to see Jesus glorified, but He had to remind her that the time for this had not yet come. Before He would appear to the world as the all-conquering Christ, He must first ascend the altar of sacrifice, and this He did at the cross of Calvary. It is a biblical principle that suffering must precede glory.

> It is a biblical principle that suffering must precede glory.

Mary understood the meaning of His words and told the servants to do whatever He commanded them (v. 5). She did not direct people to obey her or any other person; she pointed them to the Lord Jesus and told them that He was the One who should be obeyed. The teachings of Christ are given to us in the pages of the New Testament. As we read this precious book, we should remember the counsel in Mary's last recorded words in Scripture: "Whatever He says to you, do it."

Jesus Reveals His Glory

At the wedding there were six large stone pots capable of holding between sixteen and twenty-seven gallons of water apiece (v. 6). The Lord Jesus gave instructions that the waterpots should be filled with water. Notice that Jesus used facilities that were available when He was about to perform a miracle. He allowed men to provide the pots and to fill them with water, but then He did what no other human being could ever do—He changed the water into wine! It was the servants and not the disciples who filled the vessels with water, so no charge of trickery could be made. Also, the waterpots were filled to the brim, so no one could say that wine had been added to the water.

The Lord instructed the servants to draw some of the contents of the vessels and take these contents to the master of the feast. From this it is clear that the miracle had been instantaneous. The water did not become wine over a period of time, but in a second or so.

We read in verse 9 that the ruler of the feast was the one who had charge of arranging the tables and the food. When he tasted the wine, he realized something unusual had happened. He did not know where it had come from, but he discerned that the wine was of very high quality, so he immediately began to inquire of the bridegroom.

The inclusion of this incident in the life of Christ does not in itself condone the consumption of wine or other alcohol. We need to remember that wine was a commonly accepted beverage in that culture. But what should be the attitude of Christians toward wine today? Wine is sometimes prescribed for medicinal purposes, and this is entirely in accordance with New Testament teaching (1 Tim. 5:23). However, in light of the terrible abuses which abound with the intemperate use of wine and other alcoholic beverages, most Christians will want to avoid it altogether. Anyone can become addicted to strong drink, and the Scriptures condemn such usage. The way to avert this danger is to leave liquor alone. Not only that—one must always consider the effect of one's actions on others.

Jesus Reveals the True Source of Joy

The ruler of the feast knew good wine when he tasted it. It is not possible that the beverage which was served to him was merely a form of grape juice. He would not have been impressed by that. His comments draw attention to the difference between the way the Lord Jesus acted and the way people commonly acted. In this time and culture, the usual practice was to serve the best wine at the beginning of the celebration, when people could best detect and enjoy the flavor of good wine. Later on they would not be as aware of the quality of their beverage. At this particular wedding, the best wine came last. There is a spiritual application in this for us. The world commonly offers its best at the outset. It holds out its most attractive offers to young people. Then when they have wasted their lives in empty pleasure, the world offers nothing but dregs for a person's old age. The Christian life is the very opposite: it gets better all the time. Christ keeps the best wine until last.

This portion of Scripture had a very direct application to the Jewish nation at this time. There was no true joy in Judaism anymore. The people were going through a dreary round of rituals and ceremonies, but life for them was tasteless. They were strangers to divine joy. The Lord Jesus sought to teach them to put their faith in Him. He offered to turn their drab existence into fullness of joy. The water of Jewish ritual and ceremony could be turned into the wine of joyful reality in Christ if they would only welcome Him and submit to Him.

The statement in verse 11 that this was Christ's beginning miracle rules out those attributed to Jesus in His childhood found in such pseudo gospels as "The gospel of Peter," the accounts of which are little short of blasphemous in character. Foreseeing this, the Holy Spirit, as the ultimate Author of Scripture, safeguarded this period of Jesus' life and character by this little additional note.

The changing of the water into wine was a *sign*—that is, a miracle with significance, an event that "pointed" to an important fact with a spiritual meaning. The Lord's miracles proved Jesus to indeed be the Christ of God. By performing this sign, He manifested His glory. He revealed to man that He was indeed God in human flesh. His disciples believed in Him. Of course, in one sense they had believed in Him previously, but now their faith was strengthened, and they trusted Him more fully.

> **By performing this sign, Jesus manifested His glory. He revealed to man that He was indeed God in human flesh.**

"Zeal for Your house has eaten Me up" (vv. 12-17)

Jesus now left Cana and went down to Capernaum with His mother, His brothers, and His disciples. They only stayed in Capernaum a few days. Soon after, He went up to Jerusalem.

Beginning with verse 13, we have Christ's first witness to the city of Jerusalem. It is worth noting that He began and ended His public ministry by cleansing the temple at Passover time (cf. Matt. 21:12-13; Mark 11:15-18; Luke 19:45-46). The Passover was an annual feast commemorating the time when the children of Israel were delivered from slavery in Egypt and were led through the Red Sea to the wilderness, and then to the Promised Land. The first celebration of the Passover is recorded in Exodus 12. Being a devout Jew, the Lord Jesus went up to Jerusalem for this important day in the Jewish calendar year.

Coming to the temple, He found it had become a market place (v. 14). Oxen, sheep, and doves were being sold there, and money-changers were carrying on their business as well. The animals and birds were sold to the worshippers for use as sacrifices. The money-changers took the money of those who came from foreign countries and changed it into local currency so pilgrims could pay the tax to the temple. It is likely that these money-changers often took unfair advantage of those who traveled from great distances.

The whip Jesus made was probably a small lash made with strings. Notice that He did not use it as a weapon against the merchants; what the whip represented was His authority in that place. Waving the whip before Him, He cast the merchants out of the temple and upset the tables of the money-changers. He commanded those who sold doves (the offering of the poor) to leave. It was not fitting that they should make a house of merchandise out of the house of God. In all ages, God has warned His people against using religious services as a means of getting rich. There was nothing cruel or unjust in any of these actions. Rather, they simply conveyed His holiness and righteousness.

When His disciples saw what was happening, they were reminded of Psalm 69:9 where it was predicted that when the Messiah came, He would be utterly consumed with a passion for the things of God. Now they saw Jesus manifesting an intense zeal that the worship of God should be pure, and they realized that this was the One of whom the psalmist had spoken.

"Destroy this temple . . ." (vv. 18-22)

The Jews were always seeking some sign or miracle from the Lord. Despite witnessing His many miracles, however, their hearts were closed to Him, as our study in the rest of John's gospel will show. In verse 18 they questioned His right to cast the businessmen out of the temple. They demanded He perform a miracle to support His claim to be the Messiah. In answer, the Lord Jesus made an amazing statement concerning His death and resurrection: that they would destroy "this temple," but in three days He would raise it up. The deity of the Lord Jesus is again seen in this verse. Only God could say, "In three days I will raise it up."

The Jews did not understand Him. They were blind to spiritual truth. They assumed Jesus was referring to the temple in Jerusalem where they were all standing, the one built by King Herod. It had taken forty-six years to build this temple—how could any one man possibly rebuild it in three days? The Lord Jesus, however, was speaking about His own body, which was the "temple" in which all the fullness of the Godhead dwelt (Col. 2:9). Just as these Jews had shamefully treated their God-appointed temple in Jerusalem, so they would shamefully treat their God-appointed Messiah, putting Him to death in less than three years. Later on, after the Lord Jesus had been crucified and then raised from the dead, His disciples remembered He had predicted He would rise again in three days. With such a marvelous fulfillment of prophecy before their eyes, they believed both the Scripture and what Jesus had said. When it says in this verse that they believed the Scripture, it means that they believed the Old Testament predictions concerning the resurrection of God's Messiah.

We often come across truths in the Bible that are hard to understand. At some later date God will make it plain to us, even though we may not understand it now.

"He knew what was in man" (vv. 23-25)

As the result of the miracles Jesus performed in Jerusalem at the time of the Passover, many professed to believe He was the Messiah. But it was merely an outward display, similar to today where many claim to be Christians but have never truly put their faith in Christ.

> No one knows the heart of man better than Jesus Christ.

Although many believed in Him, yet Jesus did not believe in *them*. He did not entrust Himself to them. He knew they were coming to Him out of curiosity, looking for something sensational and spectacular. He knew whether their faith was real or only an imitation. "He knew all men"—He had full knowledge of what was in man and why man behaved as he did. No one knows the heart of man better than Jesus Christ. He does not need anyone to enlighten Him on this subject.

CHAPTER

4

Jesus and John the Baptist Reveal the Way into the Kingdom
John 3

"You must be born again" (vv. 1-21)

The story of Nicodemus stands in contrast to what has gone just before. Many of the Jews professed to believe in Christ, but He knew their faith was not genuine. Nicodemus was an exception. He was recognized as a teacher among his people, and Christ discerned in him an earnest desire to know the truth. Perhaps he came to the Lord for instruction so he might be able to pass that additional learning on.

Jesus Speaks to Nicodemus

The Bible does not say why Nicodemus came to Jesus at night. The most obvious explanation is that he may have felt embarrassed to be seen going to Jesus, as Jesus had by no means been accepted by the majority of the Jewish people. However, he did come to Jesus. Nicodemus acknowledged Him to be a teacher sent by God, remarking that no one could perform such miracles without God's direct help. However, learned though he was, Nicodemus did not as yet recognize Jesus as God manifest in human flesh. He was like so many today who say Jesus was a great man, a wonderful teacher, an outstanding example. All of these statements fall very far short of the full truth: Jesus was and is God.

At first sight, the response of the Lord in verse 3 does not seem to be connected with what Nicodemus had said. But it seems He was saying, "Nicodemus, you have come to Me for teaching, but what you really need is to be born again. That is where you must begin. You must be born from above, otherwise, you can never see the kingdom of God."

As a devout Jew, Nicodemus would have been looking for the Messiah to come and free the nation of Israel from the bondage of Rome. Nicodemus longed for the time when the Messiah would set up His kingdom on the earth, when the Jewish people would be chief among the nations, and when all their enemies would be destroyed. And here the Lord was informing Nicodemus that in order to enter this kingdom, a man must be born again. Just as the first birth is necessary for physical life, so a second birth is necessary for divine life. The expression "born again" may also be understood as "born from above." As the kingdom of God is spiritual in nature, its citizens must be fit to live in that spiritual sphere. And since His reign will be a righteous one, His subjects must be righteous also, and submissive to His rule. He could not reign over people who were going on in their sins.

> You must be born from above, otherwise, you can never see the kingdom of God.

Here again we see how difficult it was for people to understand the words of the Lord Jesus. Nicodemus continued to take everything in a literal sense (v. 4). He could not understand how an adult could be born again. He pondered the physical impossibility of a man entering into his mother's womb again in order to be born (cf. 1 Cor. 2:14).

Jesus Explains the Second Birth

In further explanation, the Lord Jesus told Nicodemus that he must be born of water and of the Spirit to be able to enter God's kingdom. What did He mean? Some say the Lord Jesus spoke of the necessity of baptism for salvation. However, such a teaching is contrary to the rest of the Bible. Throughout the New Testament we read that salvation is by faith in the Lord Jesus Christ alone. Baptism is intended for those who have already been saved, not as a means of salvation.

Some suggest that the water in verse 5 refers to the Word of God, the written Scriptures. Indeed, there can be no salvation apart from the Scriptures, because it is in them that God has communicated how to be saved (1 Peter 1:25). (In Ephesians 5:26 Paul uses the concept of being "washed" by the "word" to describe the ongoing work of sanctification achieved when believers obey Christ's words—not initial cleansing from sin, which is by Christ's blood.)

In Scripture, water may also refer to the Holy Spirit. In John 7:38-39, the Lord Jesus spoke of rivers of living water, and we are distinctly told that when He used the word "water," He was speaking of the Holy Spirit. If water means the Spirit in chapter 7, why can it not have the same meaning here in chapter 3? If water is taken to mean the Spirit, then it would appear on the surface that the Spirit is mentioned twice in this verse. But the word translated "and" could just as correctly be translated "even." When translated this way, the verse reads, "Unless one is born of water, even the Spirit, he cannot enter the kingdom of God." We believe that this is the correct way to translate this verse. Physical birth is not enough—there must also be spiritual birth if a man is to enter the kingdom of God. This spiritual birth is produced by the Holy Spirit of God when a person puts his faith in the Lord Jesus Christ. This interpretation is supported by the expression "born of the Spirit" found twice in verses 6 and 8.

> A spiritual birth takes place when a person believes in the Lord Jesus.

Even if Nicodemus could have been born a second time physically in some way, that would not have corrected the evil nature in him. The expression "that which is born of the flesh is flesh" means that children born of human parents are born in sin and are hopeless and helpless to save themselves. On the other hand, "that which is born of the Spirit is spirit." A spiritual birth takes place when a person believes in the Lord Jesus. When a person is born again through the Spirit, he receives a new nature and is made fit for the kingdom of God.

Jesus chided Nicodemus for being amazed at His teaching here. Nicodemus was well-versed in the Scriptures, so he should have realized the concept of and the necessity for regeneration (cf. Ezek. 37:4-6). He should have understood the inability of human nature to remedy its fallen condition. He must have realized that in order to be a subject of God's kingdom, a person must be holy, pure, and spiritual.

Jesus Illustrates the Second Birth

As He so often did, Jesus used nature to illustrate spiritual truth (v. 8). The new birth is very much like the wind. First of all, it takes place according to the will of God; it is not a power over which man has any control. Second, the new birth is invisible; you cannot see it taking place, but you can see the results of it in a person's life. When someone is saved, changes take place. The evil things he formerly loved, he now hates, and the things of God he formerly despised are now the very things he loves. Just as no one can fully understand the wind, so the new birth is a miraculous work of the Spirit of God which man is not able to comprehend fully. Moreover, the new birth, like the wind, is unpredictable. It is not possible to state just when and where it will take place.

Again, in verse 9, Nicodemus demonstrated the inability of the natural mind to enter into divine things. He was no doubt still thinking of the new birth in physical rather than spiritual terms. So he asked Jesus, "How can these things be?" The thrust of verses 10-12 is well summed up by Charles R. Erdman:

> As Nicodemus expresses his surprise or bewilderment, our Lord states that these are truths which he should have already known; they are merely "earthly things," which the Old Testament taught, and John [the Baptist] had recently proclaimed; but there are "heavenly things" concerning Jesus' own Person and work which he alone can reveal. These "heavenly things" do not concern the need and nature of the new birth, which Nicodemus should have already known, but they concern its condition, its method, even faith in a divine, crucified Saviour; they answer the eager question of Nicodemus: "How can these things be?" These last words must concern more than blind incredulity or astonishment. Nicodemus must have been willing to believe, for Christ now proceeds to reveal to him in startling fullness the divine plan of salvation. He assures Nicodemus that he [Jesus] is worthy of trust as he brings the revelation, for he is not only a human messenger "sent from God," but a divine Being, one with God, who came down from heaven, and, even as man, is in the most full and free and perfect fellowship with God.

The substance of this revelation is this: "As Moses lifted up the serpent in the wilderness, even so must the Son of Man be lifted up; that whosoever believeth may in him have eternal life."

The Lord Jesus had already told Nicodemus in verse 3 that the new birth was necessary. But how does the new birth take place? The penalty of man's sins must be met. People cannot go to heaven in their sins. The answer lay in the illustration of an incident in Israel's history: just as Moses had lifted up a serpent of brass on a pole in the wilderness when all the children of Israel had been bitten by serpents (for complaining), even so must the Son of Man be lifted up. (Read the historical event recorded in Numbers 21:4-9.) The serpents' bites were fatal, so the sinning Israelites were dying from their wounds. The people appealed to Moses to intercede with God for them. God then told Moses to make a serpent out of brass and raise it high up on a pole, visible to the whole camp. Any stricken Israelite who simply looked at the serpent was miraculously healed.

Men and women have been bitten by the viper of sin and are condemned to eternal death. The serpent of brass pictures the Lord Jesus. In the Bible, brass speaks of judgment. Jesus took our place and bore the judgment which we deserve. The pole speaks of the cross of Calvary upon which Jesus was lifted up. We are saved by looking to Him in faith—that is, by taking God at His word that Christ's death is the means by which we are saved. Whoever puts their faith in Christ, believing He died for him or her personally, is saved from eternal judgment and receives eternal life as a free gift in its place.

Regarding the rest of the chapter, another comment from Charles Erdman is worth noting here:

> The question is often raised as to whether verses 16-21 are the words of Jesus or of John. It is not a problem of supreme consequence, for whether uttered by our Lord in the presence of Nicodemus or embodying truth taught by John on other occasions, they form a fitting conclusion to this fascinating paragraph.

Jesus Is the Means of the Second Birth

John 3:16 is one of the best known verses in the entire Bible, no doubt because it states the gospel so clearly and simply. It summarizes what the Lord Jesus had been teaching Nicodemus concerning the manner by which the new birth is received. "God," we read, "so loved the world." The world here includes all mankind. God does not love men's sins or the wicked world system, but He loves all *people* and is not willing that any should perish. The way He demonstrated His love ("*so* loved," or "loved in this way") was by giving His only begotten (unique) Son. Leon Morris writes:

> **God's love is not a vague, sentimental feeling, but a love that costs.**

> The Greek construction puts some emphasis on the actuality of the gift: it is not 'God loved the world enough to give,' but 'God so loved that he gave.' His love is not a vague, sentimental feeling, but a love that costs. God gave what was most dear to him.

God has no other Son like the Lord Jesus. It was an expression of His infinite love that He would be willing to give Him for a race of rebel sinners. This does not mean that everyone is automatically saved. A person must receive what Christ has done for him before God will give him eternal life. Therefore, the words are added, "that whoever believes in Him should not perish." There is no need for anyone to perish. A way has been provided whereby all might be saved, but a person must, in an individual and conscious act, believe in Jesus Christ as his Lord and Savior. When he does this, he has eternal life as a present possession.

God is not a harsh, cruel ruler, anxious to pour out His anger on mankind (v. 17). God's heart is filled with tenderness toward man, and He has gone to the utmost cost in order to save men. He could have sent His Son into the world to condemn the world, but instead He sent Him to suffer and die that the world might be saved through Him. The work of the Lord Jesus Christ on the cross of Calvary was of such tremendous value that all sinners everywhere could be saved if they would receive Him.

It is up to each individual to decide whether he will accept the Lord Jesus or reject Him.

People either believe in Christ or not. Our eternal destiny is determined by the attitude we take toward the Son of God (v. 18). The one who trusts in Christ is not condemned, but the one who does not is condemned already. The Lord Jesus has finished the work of salvation, and now it is up to each individual to decide whether he will accept Him or reject Him. It is a terrible thing to reject such a gift of love. If a man will not believe on the Lord Jesus, God can do nothing else but condemn him. Believing in the "name" of Jesus (v. 18) is the same as believing in Him. In the Bible, the name stands for the person. If you trust His name, you trust *Him*.

Jesus was the Light who came into the world (v. 19). He was the sinless, spotless Lamb of God. But do people love Him for this? No—they resent Him. They prefer their sins to their need of a Savior from sin, and so they reject Him. Those who love sin hate the light because the light exposes their sinfulness. When Jesus was here in the world, sinful people were made uncomfortable by His presence because He revealed their awful condition by His own holiness. The best way to reveal the crookedness of one stick is to place a straight stick beside it. Coming into the world as a perfect man, Jesus Christ revealed the crookedness of all others, by comparison. If a man is truly honest before God, he will come to the Light (that is, to the Lord Jesus) in faith, realize his own utter worthlessness and sinfulness, trust the Savior for himself, and thus be born again.

"He [Jesus] must increase . . ." (vv. 22-36)

Christ's witness in the city of Jerusalem has been described. From verse 22 to the end of the chapter we have Christ testifying in Judea, where no doubt He continued preaching and teaching. As men and women came to the light, they were baptized. It would appear from this verse that Jesus Himself did the baptizing, but we learn in John 4:2 that it was done by His disciples.

John the Baptist Continues His Ministry

The John referred to in verse 23 is John the Baptist. He was still preaching his message of repentance in Judea and baptizing those Jews who were willing to repent in preparation for Christ's coming. Verse 24 is given to explain John's continued ministry and the continued response of devout Jews to it. In the near future, John would be cast into prison and beheaded for his faithful testimony (recorded in some detail by Matthew, Mark, and Luke). But in the meantime he was still diligently carrying out his commission.

From verse 25 it is clear that John's disciples became engaged in a dispute with a certain Jew about "purification." The word probably refers to baptism. The argument was whether the baptism of John was better than that of Jesus. Perhaps some of John's disciples unwisely contended that no baptism could be better than that of their master. Perhaps one of the

Pharisees tried to make John's disciples envious of Jesus and His current popularity. They came to John for a decision. They seemed to be saying to him, "If your baptism is the better, why is it that so many are leaving you and going to Jesus?" John bore witness to the Lord Jesus, and as a result of this witness, many of John's own disciples left him and began to follow Jesus.

There are two ways to understand John's reply. If he was referring to Jesus, it means that any success Jesus had indicated God's approval of Him. If John was referring to himself, he was saying that he had never pretended to be anyone great or important; he had never claimed that his baptism was superior to that of Jesus. He simply said here that he did not have anything but what he had received from heaven. We learn a life principle here: there is never reason to be proud or to seek to build up ourselves in people's esteem.

John the Baptist Acknowledges Jesus' Superiority

John reminded his disciples (v. 28) that he had pointed out time and again that he was not the Christ but simply the one sent to prepare the way for Him. They should not have been arguing over him. The Lord Jesus Christ was the bridegroom; John the Baptist was merely the friend of the Bridegroom. (We would say today that he was the "best man.") The bride does not belong to the friend of the bridegroom, but rather to the bridegroom himself. It was fitting, therefore, that the people should follow Jesus rather than John. The "bride" here refers in a general way to all who would become disciples of the Lord Jesus. In the Old Testament, Israel was spoken of as the wife of Jehovah.

Later on in the New Testament, those who are members of Christ's church are described under the figure of a bride. But here in John's gospel the word was used in a general sense to include those who left John the Baptist when Christ appeared. It did not mean either Israel or the church. John was not unhappy to lose followers; it was his great joy to listen to the voice of the Bridegroom. He was satisfied that Jesus received all the attention. His joy was fulfilled when Christ was praised and honored by people.

The entire object of John's ministry is summarized in verse 30. He labored ceaselessly to point men and women to the Lord and to make them realize His true worth. To do this he had to keep himself in the background. For a servant of Christ to seek to attract attention to himself is really a form of disloyalty. (Note the three "musts" in this chapter—for the sinner [v. 7]; for the Savior [v. 14]; and for the saint [v. 30].)

Jesus is the One who came from above and is above all. This statement in verse 31 shows His heavenly origin and supreme position. Confirming his own lowly status, John the Baptist said that he himself was of the earth—earthly—and spoke of the earth. This simply meant that, as to his birth, he was born a man of human parents. He had no heavenly rank and could not speak with the same authority as the Son of God. He was inferior to the Lord Jesus because "He who comes from heaven is above all." Christ is the supreme Sovereign of the universe. It is only proper, therefore, that people should follow Him rather than His messenger. But when the Lord Jesus spoke in verse 32, He spoke with authority. He told of what He had seen and heard. There was no possibility of error or deceit. Yet strange to say, no one received His testimony. The expression "no one" is not to be taken in an absolute sense. Some, obviously, did accept the words of the Lord Jesus. However, John was looking at mankind in general and simply stating (even predicting) man's rejection of Christ's teachings.

> If God has said something, it must be true.

By and large, comparatively few were willing to listen to the One who came down from heaven. Those who did "receive His testimony," by their acceptance set their seal on the fact that God is true. So it is today. When people accept the message of the gospel, they take sides with God against themselves and against the rest of mankind. They realize that if God has said something, it must be true. Notice how clearly this verse teaches the deity of Christ. This is just another way of saying that the testimony of Christ is the testimony of God, and to receive the one is to receive the other also.

Jesus was the One whom God sent. He spoke the words of God. To support this statement, John stated that God did not give the Spirit "by measure" to Him—that is, it was not limited in any way. The Lord Jesus Christ was anointed by the Holy Spirit of God in a way that was not true of any other person. Others have been conscious of the help of the Holy Spirit in their ministry, but no one else ever had such a Spirit-filled ministry as the Son of God.

Verse 35 records one of the seven times in John's gospel he records that the Father loves the Son. Here, that love is manifested in giving Him control over all things. Among these things over which Christ has complete charge are the destinies of human beings, as explained in the following verse. God has given His Son the power to grant everlasting life to all who put their faith in Him.

This is one of the clearest verses in the whole Bible on how a person can be saved. Salvation is not gained by keeping the Ten Commandments, obeying the Golden Rule, doing the best we can, or working our way to heaven. It is simply by believing in the Son. Remember, God is speaking. He is making a promise that can never be broken. He says clearly and distinctly that anyone who believes in His Son has everlasting life. To accept this promise is not a leap in the dark—it is to simply believe what could not possibly be false. Those who do not obey the Son of God will not see life; in fact, the wrath of God abides on them already. Our eternal destiny depends upon what we do with the Son of God. If we receive Him, God gives us eternal life as a free gift. If we reject Him, we will never enjoy everlasting life, and not only so, but God's wrath already hangs over us, ready to fall at any moment.

> **Our eternal destiny depends upon what we do with the Son of God. If we receive Him, God gives us eternal life as a free gift.**

CHAPTER

5

JESUS REVEALS HIMSELF TO THE SAMARITANS
JOHN 4:1-42

"But He needed to go through Samaria" (vv. 1-30)

In this chapter we read of Jesus having a personal conversation with another individual, but a markedly different one to Nicodemus. John sets the scene by recording in verses 1 to 3 that the Pharisees had heard that Jesus was baptizing more disciples than John and that John's popularity was evidently declining. Perhaps they had attempted to use this fact to stir up envy and contention between the disciples of John and those of the Lord Jesus. Actually, Jesus Himself did not perform the act of baptism; this was done by His disciples. However, the people were baptized as followers or disciples of the Lord. By leaving Judea and journeying into Galilee, Jesus would prevent the Pharisees from succeeding in their efforts to cause divisions. But there is another significant fact in this verse: Judea was the headquarters of the Jewish people, whereas Galilee was a Gentile region. Jesus knew that the Jewish people were already rejecting Him and His testimony, and so here He turns to the Gentile people.

Samaria was on the direct route from Judea to Galilee (v. 4), but few Jews ever traveled this way. The region of Samaria was so despised by the Jewish people that they often took a very roundabout route through Perea in order to go north into Galilee. Thus, when it says that the Lord Jesus "had to" go through Samaria, the thought is not so much that He was compelled to do so geographically, but rather because there were many spiritually needy souls in Samaria. Traveling into Samaria, Jesus came to a little village named Sychar (4:5). Not far from that village was a piece of ground which Jacob had given to his son Joseph, as recorded in Genesis 48:22. A spring known as Jacob's well was in this area. It is one of the few biblical sites which can be identified quite positively today.

It was about noontime ("the sixth hour") when Jesus reached the well. He was weary as a result of His long walk, so He sat down on the well. As God, He could never become tired, but as a man, He could. The truth that God could come down into the world and live as a man among men is a mystery which surpasses our understanding.

> The truth that God could come down into the world and live as a man among men is a mystery which surpasses our understanding.

Jesus Speaks to a Woman of Samaria

While He was sitting by the well, a woman came out from the village to draw water (v. 7). Noon was a very unusual time for women to do this, as it was the hottest part of the day. But this woman was a very immoral one, and it may have been her practice to come at this time because she knew no other women would be there. Of course, the Lord Jesus knew she would be at the well at this time. He knew she was a soul in need, and it appears that He determined to meet her and to rescue her from her sinful life.

In verse 7 and the verses to follow, we find the master soul-winner at work, and we will do well to study the methods He used to bring this woman to a sense of her need and then to offer to her the solution to her problem. Jesus opened the conversation by asking a favor. Wearied with His journey, He desired a drink. His disciples had gone to Sychar to purchase some food, and to all outward appearance, Jesus had no means for getting water from the well (v. 8).

The woman recognized Jesus as a Jew and was amazed that He would speak to her, a Samaritan (v. 9). (It was also extremely unusual for men to speak with women in public.) The Samaritans claimed descent from Jacob, and looked upon themselves as true Israelites. Actually, they were of mixed Jewish and heathen descent. Mount Gerizim (a mountain in Samaria, clearly visible to the Lord and to this woman as they talked together) had been adopted by them as their official place of worship. The Jewish people disliked the Samaritans deeply. They considered them half-breeds. That is why this woman said, "How is it that You, being a Jew, ask a drink from me, a Samaritan woman?" Little did she realize that she was speaking to her Creator, and that His love rose above all the petty distinctions of humankind.

Jesus Offers Living Water

We see in verse 10 that by asking a favor, the Lord aroused her interest and curiosity. If she had realized that the One to whom she was talking was God manifest in the flesh, she would have asked Him for a blessing, and He would have given her living water. From verse 11 we see the woman could only think of literal water and of the impossibility of His getting it without the necessary equipment. She completely (and understandably) failed to understand His words.

Her confusion deepened when she thought of the patriarch Jacob, who had given this well (v. 12). He himself had used it, as well as his children and his cattle. Now here, centuries later, was a weary traveler who asked for a drink from Jacob's well and yet who claimed to be able to give something better than the water in the well. If He had something better, why was He asking for water from this well? So the Lord began to explain the difference between the literal water of Jacob's well and the water He would give. Whoever drank of this water would thirst again—surely the woman could understand this. She had been coming out day after day to draw from the well, yet the need was never completely met. And so it is with all the "wells" of this world. Men seek their pleasure and satisfaction in earthly things, but these things are not able to quench the thirst of the human heart. The "water" Jesus gives truly satisfies (v. 14), not only blessing and filling the heart, but overflowing it as well. The metaphor presents a vivid contrast. All that earth can provide is not sufficient to fill the human heart. The pleasures of this world are for a few short years, but the pleasures which Christ provides go on into everlasting life.

> **The "water" Jesus gives truly satisfies.**

When the woman heard of this marvelous water, she immediately wanted it. But she was still thinking of literal water. She did not realize that the water of which the Lord Jesus had been speaking was spiritual, that He was referring to all the blessings which come to a human soul through placing personal faith in Him.

Jesus Confronts the Woman with Her Sin

But in verse 16 there is an abrupt change in the conversation. The Lord Jesus told her to go and call her husband. Why? Because before this woman could partake of living water that issued in eternal life, she needed to acknowledge she was a sinner. She must repent, confessing her guilt and shame. The Lord Jesus knew all about the sinful life she had lived, and He was going to lead her, step by step, to acknowledge it for herself.

Only those who know themselves to be lost can be saved. We are all lost, but not all of us are willing to admit it. In seeking to win men and women for Christ, we must never avoid the sin question. People must face the fact that they are dead in trespasses and sins (Eph. 2:1), that they need a Savior, that they cannot save themselves. Jesus is the Savior they need.

> People must face the fact that they are dead in trespasses and sins, that they need a Savior, that they cannot save themselves. Jesus is the Savior they need.

We see in verse 17 that at first the woman tried to withhold the truth without telling a lie. She said, "I have no husband." Perhaps in a strictly legal sense her statement was true, but she was trying to hide the fact that she was living in sin with a man who was not her husband. The Lord Jesus, as God, knew all this. This is why He says in verse 18, "You are right in saying, 'I have no husband.'" He knew all about her. The Lord never used His knowledge to needlessly expose or shame a person. But He did use it, as here, in order to deliver a person from the bondage of sin. How startled she must have been when He recited her past history! She had had five husbands, and the man with whom she was now living was not her husband.

There is some difference of opinion among Bible scholars about this verse. Some teach that the woman's five previous husbands had either died or had deserted her, and that there was nothing sinful in her relationships with them. Whether or not this is so, it is clear from the latter part of the verse that this woman was an adulteress. "He whom you now have is not your husband." This is the important point. The woman was sinning, and until she was willing to acknowledge this, the Lord could not bless her with the living water.

With her life laid open before her, the woman realized the One speaking to her was no ordinary person. However, she did not realize yet that He was God. She thought He was a prophet, that is, a spokesman for God (v. 19).

Jesus Discusses Worship

It seems now that the woman had become convicted of her sins, and so she tried to change the subject by introducing a question concerning the proper place for worship. "Our fathers worshiped on this mountain," she said, pointing to Mount Gerizim. Then she reminded the Lord (unnecessarily) that the Jewish people claimed Jerusalem as the proper place of worship. He did not avoid her comment; instead, He used it to impart further spiritual truth. He told her that the time was coming when neither Jerusalem nor Gerizim would be the place of worship. In Old Testament times, Jerusalem was appointed by God as *the* city where worship should be offered to Him. Devout Jews would come to the temple in Jerusalem with their sacrifices and offerings. Of course, in the gospel age, this is no longer so. God does not have any certain place on earth where people must go to worship. The Lord explained this more fully in the verses to follow.

When the Lord said in verse 22, "You worship what you do not know," He condemned the Samaritan mode of worship. His statement stands in marked contrast with religious teachers who say that all religions are good and lead to heaven (or some kind of eternal bliss) at last. Jesus informed this woman that God had neither authorized nor approved the Samaritan form of worship. It had been invented by man and carried on without His sanction. This was not so with the worship of the Jews. The Jewish people were His chosen earthly people. He had given them instructions on the way to worship Him. "Salvation is from the Jews," said the Lord. The Jewish people were appointed by God to be His messengers and to write God's Holy Scriptures. In addition, it was through the Jewish nation the Messiah was given, and He was born of a Jewish mother.

Next, Jesus informed the woman that, with His coming, God no longer designated a certain place on earth for worship (v. 23). Those who believe in the Lord Jesus can worship God at any time and in any place. True worship means that no matter where he is, a believer can, by faith, enter the presence of God to praise and worship Him. Jesus told this woman that from now on, worship of the Father that was acceptable to Him would be in "spirit and truth." The attitude of the worshiper as well as the content (i.e. what he did and said) were the issue. The Jews had reduced worship to outward forms and ceremonies, but theirs was not a worship of the spirit—it was outward, not inward. Their bodies might be bowed down on the ground, but their hearts were not right before God.

The Samaritans, on the other hand, had a form of worship which was even more false—it had no scriptural authority at all. They had formatted their own religion and were carrying out ordinances of their own invention. Thus, when the Lord Jesus said that worship acceptable to the Father must be in spirit and in truth, He was rebuking both Jews and Samaritans. But He was also informing them that it was now possible for people to draw near to God through Him in true and sincere worship. The Father "is seeking such to worship Him." Think about this! The Father seeks worshipers. God desires the adoration of His people. Does He receive this from you?

> The Father seeks worshipers. God desires the adoration of His people. Does He receive this from you?

The statement in verse 24 that "God is Spirit" defines God's being. He is not a mere man, subject to all the errors and limitations of humanity. Neither is He confined to any one place at any one time. He is an invisible person who is present in all places at one and the same time. He is all-knowing, all-powerful, and perfect in all His ways. It is therefore incongruous to worship such a God when inwardly one's life is corrupt. There must be no idea that in going through a series of rituals, God is thereby pleased. Even if God instituted those rituals Himself, He still insists that man approach Him with a broken and a contrite heart.

While the woman of Samaria was listening to the Lord, her mind had gone to thinking of the coming Messiah (v. 25). The Spirit of God had stirred up within her a desire that the Messiah should come. She expressed confidence that when He did come, He would teach them all things. In this statement, she showed a very clear understanding of one of the great purposes of Christ's coming.

What the Lord Jesus really said to her in reply was, "I who speak to you am He." The word "He" is not a part of the original text. The sentence might perhaps be clearer with the word *He* included, yet there is a deep significance to the actual words of the Lord. He used one of the names which God applied to Himself in the Old Testament. He said, "I AM is speaking to you," or, in other words, "Jehovah is the One who is speaking to you." He was announcing to her the startling truth that the One who was speaking to her was the Messiah for whom she had been looking, and that He was also God Himself.

When the disciples returned from Sychar, they found Jesus deep in conversation with this woman. Going on outward appearances alone, they were surprised He would speak with her, not only because she was a Samaritan, but because she was female.

The woman left her water pot! It symbolized the things she had used to satisfy her deepest longings. They had all failed. Now that she had found the Lord Jesus, she had no more need for the things which had formerly been so prominent in her life. She not only left her water pot, but she went into the city. One characteristic of a newly saved person is their concern for the souls of others.

We see from verse 29 that her witness was simple but effective. She invited the townspeople to come and see the man who told her "all things" that she had ever done. Also, she aroused within their hearts the possibility that this man might indeed be the Messiah. In her own mind there could be little doubt, because He had already announced Himself to her as the Christ. But she raised the question in their minds so that they might go to Jesus and find out for themselves. Undoubtedly this woman was well known in the village for her sin and shame. How startling it must have been for the people to see her standing in the public places now, bearing public witness to the Lord Jesus Christ! The testimony of the woman was effective. The people left their homes and their work and went out to find Jesus.

> **One characteristic of a newly saved person is their concern for the souls of others.**

"The fields . . . are already white for harvest" (vv. 31-38)

The disciples were now back, so they encouraged the Lord to eat. Apparently they were not aware of the momentous events that were taking place. At this historic moment when a Samaritan city was being introduced to the Lord of Glory, their thoughts rose no higher than food for their bodies (v. 32). The Lord Jesus had found His nourishment and support in winning worshipers to His Father. Compared to this joy, physical food was of little importance to Him. We get what we go after in life. The disciples were interested in food: they went into the village to get food, and they came back with it. Jesus was interested in souls. He was interested in saving men and women from sin, and giving them the water of everlasting life. He, too, found what He went after. What are you interested in?

Because of their earthly outlook, the disciples failed to understand the meaning of the Lord's words. They concluded that someone must have come along and given Jesus some food (v. 34). Again, He tried to turn their attention from the material to the spiritual. His "food" was to do God's will and to finish the work God had given Him to do. Not that He refrained from eating physical food; rather, the great aim and object of His life was to do God's will.

Jesus Teaches His Disciples

Perhaps the disciples had been talking together about the coming harvest (v. 35). Or perhaps it was a common saying among the Jews, "Four months between seed time and harvest." At any rate, Jesus used the physical fact of harvest to teach a spiritual lesson. The disciples should not think that harvest time was still far off. They could not afford to spend their lives in quest of food and clothing, rationalizing that God's work could be done later on. They must grasp the fact that the fields were already white for harvest. The fields here, of course, refer to the world. At this very moment, Jesus was in the midst of a harvest field containing the souls of Samaritan men and women. He was telling the disciples that a great work of in-gathering lay before them, and that they should give themselves to it immediately and diligently. So today, the Lord would say to believers, "Lift up your eyes, and look on the fields." As we spend time contemplating the great need of the world, the Lord will lay upon our hearts a burden for the lost souls around us. Then it will be up to us to go forth for Him, seeking to bring in the sheaves of ripened grain.

In verse 36 we find the Lord Jesus instructing the disciples concerning the work to which they were called. He had chosen them to be reapers. They would not only earn wages in this life, but they would gather fruit for eternity as well. Service for Christ has many rewards at the present time. But in a coming day, reapers will have the additional joy of seeing souls in heaven because of their faithfulness in proclaiming the gospel message. In heaven, both the sower and the reaper will rejoice together. In natural life, the field must first be prepared for the seed, and then the seed must be sown in it. Later on, the grain is harvested. Thus it is in the spiritual life also. First of all, the message must be preached. Then it must be watered with prayer. But when the harvest season comes, all who have had a part in the work will rejoice together.

In this, Christ recognized a fulfillment of the proverb that was common in that day: "One sows and another reaps." Some Christians are called upon to preach the gospel for many years without seeing much fruit for their labor. Others step in at the end of those years, and many souls turn to Christ. The Lord was sending His disciples into areas that had already been prepared by others. Throughout the Old Testament period, the prophets had foretold the coming of the gospel era and of the Messiah. Then, too, John the Baptist came as Christ's forerunner, seeking to prepare the hearts of the people to receive Him. The Lord Himself had sown the seed in Samaria and prepared a harvest for the reapers. Now the disciples were about to step into the harvest field, and the Lord wanted them to know that, while they would have the joy of seeing many turning to Christ, they should understand they were entering into the labors of others. Very few souls are ever saved through the ministry of a single person. Most people hear the gospel many times before they turn to the Lord. Therefore, the one who finally leads a person to Christ should not exalt himself as if he were the only instrument God used in this marvelous work.

"This is indeed the Christ" (vv. 39-42)

> Be simple, bold, and direct in your witness for Christ.

As a result of the simple and forthright testimony of this Samaritan woman, many of her people believed in the Lord Jesus. All she said was, "He told me all things that I ever did," and yet that was sufficient to bring others to the Savior. This should be an encouragement to each of us to be simple, bold, and direct in our witness for Christ. The reception given to the Lord Jesus by the Samaritans stood in marked contrast to that of the Jews. The Samaritans seemed to have some real appreciation of this wonderful person, and they invited Him to stay with them. As a result, the Lord stayed two days. How privileged this city of Sychar was, that it should entertain the Messiah during this period of time!

No two conversions are exactly alike. Some believed because of the testimony of the woman (v. 41). Many more believed because of the words of Christ Himself. The principle to note here is that God uses various means in bringing sinners to Himself (v. 42). It is wonderful to hear these Samaritans bearing such clear testimony about Christ. They had complete assurance of salvation based not upon the word of a woman, but upon the words of the Lord Jesus Himself. Having heard Him and believed His words, the Samaritans had come to know that He was indeed the Christ, the Savior of the world. Only the Holy Spirit could have given them this insight. The Jewish people, of course, thought that the Messiah would be for the Jews alone. But the Samaritans realized that the benefits of Christ's mission would extend to all the world.

CHAPTER

6

JESUS MINISTERS TO INDIVIDUALS IN GALILEE AND JERUSALEM
JOHN 4:43–5:23

"The man believed the word that Jesus spoke to him" (4:43-54)

After spending the two days among the Samaritans, the Lord Jesus turned His footsteps northward into Galilee.

Verse 44 seems to present a difficulty. It states that the reason for Christ's moving from Samaria to Galilee was that "a prophet has no honor in his own country." And yet Galilee *was* His own country, since Nazareth was a city located in that region. Perhaps the meaning is that Jesus went into some part of Galilee other than Nazareth. In any case, the statement is true that a person is not usually appreciated as much in his own home town as he is in other places. Certainly, the Lord Jesus was not appreciated by His own people as He should have been.

Jesus Receives a Favorable Reception in Galilee

When Jesus returned to Galilee, He was given a favorable reception because the people had seen the things He had done at the feast in Jerusalem (v. 45). Obviously, the Galileans referred to here were Jews. They had gone down to Jerusalem to worship. They had seen the Lord there and witnessed some of His mighty works. Now they were willing to have Him in their midst in Galilee, not because they acknowledged Him to be the Son of God, but because they were curious about the One who was arousing so much comment everywhere He went.

The village of Cana was honored again by a visit from Christ (v. 46). On the first visit, some there had seen Him turn the water into wine. Now they were to witness another mighty miracle by Him, the effect of which would extend to Capernaum.

The son of a certain nobleman from Capernaum (13 miles away) was sick. This man was undoubtedly a Jew employed by Herod Antipas, the Rome-appointed king. He had heard that Jesus had now returned to Galilee from Judea. He must have had some faith in Jesus' ability to heal because he came directly to Him and pleaded that He would restore his dying son. In this sense, he seems to have had a greater trust in Him than most of his fellow countrymen.

Speaking not only to the nobleman but to the Jewish people in general (plural "you"), the Lord reminded them of a national characteristic, that they desired to see miracles before they would believe (v. 48). Generally speaking, Jesus was not as pleased with a faith based on miracles as He was with faith based on His word alone. It is more honoring to Him to believe a thing simply because He said it than because of some visible proof. It is characteristic of man that he wants to see before he believes. But the principle that John draws our attention to several times in the gospel is that we should first believe, and then we will see.

> The principle that John draws our attention to is that we should first believe, and then we will see.

The words "signs" and "wonders" both refer to miracles. "Signs" are miracles that have a deep meaning or significance. "Wonders" are miracles that cause people to be amazed by their supernatural qualities. The latter term is only used here in John's gospel.

Jesus Enables the Nobleman's Faith to Increase

The nobleman, with the persistence of faith, believed that Jesus could do his son good, and he wanted a visit from Him more than anything else. In one sense, his faith was defective: he thought that Jesus would have to be at the boy's bedside before He could heal him. However, Jesus did not rebuke him for this, but rewarded him for the measure of faith he *did* exhibit. Jesus' aim was to deepen his faith.

In verse 50 we see the man's faith growing. He exercised what little faith he had, and the Lord gave him more. Jesus sent him home with the promise, "Your son lives." The son had been healed! Without any miracle or visible proof, the man believed the word of the Lord Jesus and started for home. That is faith in action! As he was nearing home, his servants came out to meet him with the news that his son was well. The man was not at all shocked by this announcement. He had believed the promise of the Lord Jesus, and having believed, he would now see the evidence. He had believed the promise of Jesus but apparently did not believe the cure would be instantaneous. He asked the servants as to the time when his son began to get better. Their answer revealed that the healing was not gradual; it had taken place instantly. There could now be not the slightest trace of doubt about this wonderful miracle. At the seventh hour of the previous day, Jesus had said to the nobleman in Cana, "Your son lives." At the very same hour in the village of Capernaum, the son had been healed, and the fever had left him. Author Warren Wiersbe describes the progress of the man's faith this way: from crisis faith (v. 47), to confident faith (v. 50), to confirmed faith (v. 53), to contagious faith (v. 53).

From this the nobleman learned that it was not necessary for Jesus to be bodily present in order to work a miracle or answer prayer. This should encourage all Christians in their prayer life. We have a mighty God who hears our requests and who is able to work out His purposes in any part of the world at any time. The nobleman believed, along with his entire household. It is apparent from this and from similar verses in the New Testament that God loves to see families united in Christ. It is not His will that there should be divided families in heaven. He takes care to record the fact that the whole household believed in His Son.

The healing of the nobleman's son was not the second miracle in the Lord's entire ministry up to this point (v. 54). Rather, it was the second miracle He performed in Galilee after He had left Judea. Jesus had met with unbelief in Judea, and with belief in Galilee.

"Do you want to be made well?" (5:1-9)

Chapter 5 opens with the information that one of the Jewish feasts in Jerusalem was due. This may have been the Feast of Passover, but it is impossible to be sure. Jesus was born into the world as a Jew, and as such He was obedient to the laws that God had made for the Jewish people. He therefore went to Jerusalem for the Feast, obedient to the very laws that He had created.

In the city of Jerusalem there was a pool named Bethesda. The word *Bethesda* means "house of mercy" or "house of pity." This pool was located by the sheep market (or by the sheep gate). Around the pool there were five porches or large open spaces capable of holding a number of people.

Apparently the pool of Bethesda was known as a place where miracles of healing occurred (v. 3). Whether these miracles took place throughout the year or only at certain times, such as on feast days, we do not know. Many people surrounded the pool; they were there hoping to be cured. The infirmities listed in verse 3 comprise a composite picture of sinful man in his helplessness, blindness, lameness, and uselessness. These people, suffering from the effect of original sin in their bodies, were waiting for the moving of the water. Their hearts must have been filled with longing to be freed from their sicknesses, and they earnestly desired to find healing.

The narrative here in verse 4 does not satisfy our curiosity as to how this phenomenon originated. We are simply told that at a certain time an angel came down and "stirred up" the water. The first person who was able to get into the water at that time was healed of his sickness. What a pitiful sight it must have been to see so many people in need of help struggling to get into the water, and yet only one was able to benefit from the healing power. (Note that the latter part of verse 3 and all of verse 4 are omitted from many versions of the Bible. Some scholars suggest that the agitation of the water was caused by springs at the bottom of the pool, and that popular opinion attributed the agitation to an angel.)

Jesus Heals on the Sabbath

In verse 5 we discover that one of the men waiting by the pool had been an invalid for thirty-eight years. He had been in this condition even before Jesus was born! In loving compassion, Jesus asked him in verse 6, "Do you want to be made well?" Jesus knew this was the greatest longing of the man's heart, but He wanted to draw out from the man an admission of his own helplessness and of his desperate need for healing. It is the same with salvation. The Lord knows we need to be saved, but He waits to hear the confession from our own lips that we are lost and that we need to receive Him as our Savior. We are not saved by our own will, yet the

> The Lord knows we need to be saved, but He waits to hear the confession from our own lips that we are lost and that we need to receive Him as our Savior.

human will must be exercised before God saves a soul. The answer of the sick man was pathetic. For years he had lain by the pool, waiting to get in, but every time the waters were stirred up, there was no one to help him. Every time he would try to get in, someone always arrived ahead of him. This reminds us how disappointed we are when we depend on our fellow man to save us from our sins.

> The Lord Jesus never tells a person to do a thing without giving him the power to do it.

The man's bed was a pad or a light mattress. Jesus told him to rise, to carry this pad, and to walk. When we are saved, we are not only told to rise, but to walk. The Lord Jesus gives us healing from sin, and then He expects us to walk in a manner worthy of Him. The Lord Jesus never tells a person to do a thing without giving him the power to do it. Even as He spoke, new life and power flowed into the body of this invalid. He was healed immediately; it was not a gradual recovery. Limbs that had been useless or weak for years now throbbed with strength. Then he immediately obeyed the word of the Lord. The man took up his mat and walked. What a thrill it must have been for him to do this after thirty-eight years of sickness!

This miracle took place on the Sabbath. The Sabbath, of course, was the seventh day of the week—our Saturday. The Jewish people were forbidden to do any work on the Sabbath day. This man was a Jew, and yet at the instruction of the Lord Jesus he did not hesitate to carry his mattress despite Jewish restrictions regarding the day.

"The Jews persecuted Jesus, and sought to kill Him" (5:10-18)

When the Jewish people (that is, their leaders) saw the man carrying his bed on the Sabbath, they challenged him. These people were very strict and harsh in carrying out their religious observances and clung rigidly to the letter of the Law, but they had little mercy and compassion for others. The healed man gave a very simple answer in verse 11. He said that the One who cured him told him to take up his bed and walk. Anyone who had the power to heal a man who had been sick for thirty-eight years ought to be obeyed, even if he told a person to carry his bed on the Sabbath! The healed man did not really know at this time who Jesus was; he spoke of Him in a very general way, and yet with real gratitude.

Naturally these religious leaders wanted to find out who dared tell this man to break the Sabbath, the violation of which demanded stoning. But it was impossible for the man to point Him out because Jesus had slipped away among the crowd that had gathered.

In all four gospels we read of occasions when Christ performed a miracle of healing on a Sabbath day or did something not in line with the Jews' legalistic view of the Law. Whenever He did so, He stirred up the anger and hostility of the Jewish leaders. They began to pursue Him and to seek His life (e.g. Mark 3:6).

Some time later Jesus found the healed man in the temple. The man had probably gone there to thank God for the wonderful miracle that had taken place in his life. Jesus reminded him (v. 14) that he had been highly favored and was therefore under solemn obligation. Privilege always brings with it responsibility. "See, you have been made well. Sin no more, lest a worse thing come upon you." It appears that this man's sickness was a result of sin in his life. This is not true of all sickness. Many times illness in a person's life has no direct connection with any sin he has committed. Infants, for instance, may be sick before they are old enough to sin knowingly. "Sin no more," said Jesus, expressing God's standard of holiness. If He had said "Sin as little as possible," He would not have been God, for God cannot condone sin in any degree. Then the warning was added, "lest [in case] a worse thing come upon you." Jesus was conveying to the man that sin has far more terrible results than physical sickness. Those who die in their sins are condemned to eternal wrath and anguish.

It is a more serious thing to sin against grace than against law. The Lord Jesus had shown wonderful love and mercy to this man. It would be a poor response to carry on in the same kind of sinful life which had led to his illness. The man wanted to pay tribute to Jesus (v. 15), but the Jews were not impressed—their chief desire was to apprehend Jesus and destroy Him (v. 16).

We observe here an exposure of the wicked heart of man. Christ Jesus had come and had performed a great act of healing, and these Jews were infuriated. They resented the fact that the miracle took place on the Sabbath. They were cold-blooded religionists, more interested in ceremonial observances than in the blessing and welfare of their fellowman. They did not realize that the very One who originally ordained the Sabbath was the One who now performed an act of mercy on this day. In any case, Jesus had *not* broken the Sabbath: the Law forbade menial work on that day, but it did not prohibit the performance of acts of necessity or of mercy.

Having finished the work of creation in six days, God had rested on the seventh day—the Sabbath. However, when sin entered into the world, God's rest was disturbed. He would now work ceaselessly to bring men and women, boys and girls, back into fellowship with Himself. He would provide a means of redemption. He would send out the gospel message to every generation. Thus from the time of Adam's fall until now, God has been working constantly, and He is still working. The same was true of the Lord Jesus. He was engaged in His Father's business, and His love and grace could not be confined to only six days of the week (v. 17).

Verse 18 is important to note. It tells us that the Jews became more determined than ever to kill Jesus. He had not only broken the Sabbath (in their view), but claimed equality with God by speaking of God as His Father. To them, this was terrible blasphemy. Actually, of course, it was the simple truth. The Lord Jesus stated His equality with God in even more positive terms in the verses that follow. As J. S. Baxter puts it: "He claims equality in seven particulars: (1) in working (v. 19); (2) in knowing (v. 20); (3) in resurrecting (v. 21 with vv. 28-29); (4) in judging (v. 22 with v. 27); (5) in honor (v. 23); (6) in regenerating (v. 24); and (7) in self-existence (v. 26)."

"The Son can do nothing of Himself . . ." (5:19-23)

Christ now claimed to be so closely united with God the Father that He could not act independently. He did not mean that He didn't have the power to do anything by Himself, but that He was so closely united with the Father that He could only do the very things that His Father was doing. He is not independent of the Father, though He is fully equal with Him.

The Lord Jesus intended the Jews to think of Him as equal with God. It would be absurd for a mere man to claim to do the very things that God Himself does. Jesus claims to see what the Father is doing. In order to make such a claim, He must have continual access to the Father and complete knowledge of what is going on in heaven. Not only so, but Jesus claims to do the very things which He sees the Father doing. This is certainly an assertion of His equality with God. He is both omniscient and omnipotent.

It is a special mark of the Father's love for His Son that He shows Him all that He Himself does (v. 20). Jesus not only saw these things; He had the power to perform them as well. Then He went on to say that God would show Him "greater works" than these so that the people might marvel—those greater works being giving life and judging (vv. 21-22). Leon Morris's commentary on verse 21 is:

> "Just as the Father takes dead bodies and raises them into new life (Deut. 32:39; 1 Sam. 2:6; 2 Kings 5:7), so the Son takes men who, though their bodies are alive, are yet in a state of death, and raises them into spiritual life. Notice the significance of 'whom He will.' Men may not command this miracle. The Son gives life where He, not man, chooses."

Could this ever be said of Him if He were a mere man? To ask the question is to answer it.

According to the New Testament, God the Father has committed the work of judgment to His Son (cf. Acts 17:31). In order for the Lord Jesus to do this work, He must, of course, have absolute knowledge and perfect righteousness. He must be able to discern the thoughts and motives of men's hearts. The Judge of all the earth stood before these Jews asserting His authority, and yet they did not recognize Him!

Here in verse 23 we have the reason, the purpose, why God has given authority to His Son to give spiritual life to men and to judge the world: so they will honor the Son, even as they honor the Father. This is a most important statement, and one of the clearest testimonies in the Bible of the deity of the Lord Jesus Christ. Throughout the Bible we are taught that God alone is to be worshipped and He will not share the honor due to Him with another (e.g. Isa. 42:8, 10-12). In the Ten Commandments, the people were forbidden to have any god but the one true God. Now we are taught that everyone should honor the Son even as they honor the Father. Leon Morris comments, "The inherent dignity of the Son and His intimate relationship to the Father make the dishonoring of Him a very serious matter indeed." The only conclusion we can come to from this verse is that Jesus Christ is God.

Many people who claim to worship God deny that Jesus Christ is God. They say He was a good man, or more godlike than any other man who ever lived. But this verse puts Him on an absolute equal footing with God and requires that people give Him the same honor they give to God the Father. If someone does not honor the Son, then he does not honor the Father. If you have never realized before who Jesus Christ is, then read this verse carefully, remember that it is holy Scripture, and accept the glorious truth that Jesus Christ is God manifest in the flesh.

CHAPTER

7

JESUS DEFENDS HIS GOD-GIVEN AUTHORITY
JOHN 5:24-47

"He who hears My word . . ." (vv. 24-29)

In the preceding verses in John 5, we learned that Christ had the power to give life and that the work of judgment had been committed to Him as well. Now in verse 24 we learn how a man may receive spiritual life from Him and escape the judgment of a holy God against his sin.

Jesus Speaks of Eternal Life

John 5:24 is a favorite gospel verse of many. Multitudes have become possessors of eternal life through embracing its message personally. The Lord Jesus began with the words, *"Most assuredly,"* drawing attention to the importance of what He was about to say. Then He added the very personal announcement, *"I say to you."* Although the pronoun "you" is plural, His audience was (and is) made up of individuals, so it is not unreasonable to hear Christ speaking to each of us personally here.

"He who hears My word." To hear the word of Jesus means to receive it, believe it, and obey it. Many people hear the gospel preached but do not respond to it. The Lord is saying here that a person must accept His teaching as divine and believe that He is indeed the Savior.

"And believes in Him who sent Me." It is a matter of believing God. This does not mean that a person is saved simply by believing *in* God, or in God alone. Many profess to believe in God yet have never been converted. The

thought is that one must believe that God sent His Son to be our Savior. *He must believe what God says about the Lord Jesus*—namely, that He is the only Savior and that He died as our Substitute on Calvary's cross.

"Has everlasting life." It does not say that the believer *will have* eternal life, but that he has it right now. Eternal life is the life of the Lord Jesus Christ. It is a quality of life. It is the life the Savior imparts to those who believe in Him. It is the spiritual life received when a man is born again in contrast to the natural life that he received at his physical birth.

"And shall not come into judgment." The believer is free from the condemnation that was his lot as a sinner when he was born into a condemned world. Christ made this claim in anticipation of the day He Himself would pay the penalty for the believer's sins on the cross, and He knew that God would not demand the payment of this penalty twice. Christ has finished the work, and nothing can be added to it. The Christian will never be punished for his sins. (There are other verses which teach that a believer will one day stand before the judgment seat of Christ, such as Romans 14:10; 2 Corinthians 5:10. However, the question of punishment will not be brought up at that time. That question was settled at Calvary. At the judgment seat of Christ, the believer's life and service will be reviewed, and he will either receive rewards or suffer loss. It will not be then a question of his soul's salvation, but of his life's fruitfulness.)

"But has passed from death into life." The one who has trusted Christ has passed out of a state of spiritual death into one of spiritual life. Before conversion, he was dead in trespasses and sins (Eph. 2:1). He was dead as far as fellowship with his Creator was concerned. When he put his faith in Jesus Christ, the Spirit of God came to indwell him and he became a possessor of eternal life.

Jesus Speaks of His Authority over Life and Judgment

Here in verse 25 Jesus uses the expression "most assuredly" for the third time (and for the seventh time so far in this gospel). When the Lord said that *the hour* was coming and now *is,* He was saying that *the time* was coming, and had arrived already. The time referred to was His coming onto the stage of history. Who are the dead spoken of in this verse? Who is it who would hear the voice of the Son of God and live? Although the Lord did raise some physically from the dead during His public ministry, the verse has a wider meaning than this: the dead are those who are dead in their sins. They hear the voice of the Son of God when the gospel is preached. When they accept the message and receive the Savior, they pass from death to life.

Verse 26 explains how a person can receive life from the Lord Jesus. Just as the Father is the Source and Giver of life, so He has decreed that the Son, too, should have life in Himself and should be able to give it to others. This is a statement of the deity of Christ and of His equality with the Father. It cannot be said of any man that he has life in himself. Life was *given* to each one of us, but it was never given to God or to Christ. From all eternity, the members of the Trinity have had life indwelling them. That life never had a beginning or came from a source outside of themselves.

Furthermore, God has given Christ authority to be the Judge of the world. This power to judge has been given to Jesus because He is the Son of man. The Lord is called both Son of God and Son of man. The title *Son of God* reminds us that Jesus Christ is one of the persons of the Godhead. As the Son, He is equal with both the Father and the Holy Spirit, and as the Son, He gives life. But He is also the *Son of man*. He came into the world as a man, lived here among human beings. He was rejected and crucified when He came into the world as a man. When He comes again, He will come to judge His enemies and to be honored in this same world where He was once so cruelly treated. Because He is both God and man, He is perfectly qualified to be Judge.

Undoubtedly, while Christ was making these strong claims to be equal with God the Father, the Jews who were listening were amazed at His statements (v. 28). He knew, of course, what thoughts were going through their minds, and so He told them that they should not marvel at these things. Then He went on to reveal to them a more startling truth: in a time yet future, all of those whose bodies are lying in the grave will hear His voice. How foolish it would be for anyone who was not God to predict such an event! Only God could ever support such a statement.

All the dead will one day be raised. Some will be raised to life, others to condemnation. Every living person in the past, present, or future falls into one of these two classes. If this was the only verse in the Bible on the subject of resurrection, one might conclude that all the dead will be raised at the same time. However, we know from other portions of Scripture, particularly Revelation chapter 20, that a period of at least 1,000 years will elapse between the two resurrections. The first resurrection is the resurrection of those who have been saved through faith in Christ. The second resurrection includes all who have died as unbelievers.

Verse 29 does not teach that people who have done good will be saved because of their good deeds, while those who have done evil will be condemned because of their wicked lives. Good works are not the root of salvation, but the fruit of it. They are the effect, not the cause. The expression "those who have done evil" describes those who have never put their faith in the Lord Jesus to save them, and consequently whose lives have been evil in God's sight. These will be raised to stand before God in order to be sentenced to eternal doom.

The thought of verse 30 is that the Lord is so closely united with God the Father that He could not act by Himself. He could not do anything on His own authority. There was no trace of willfulness in Christ Jesus. He acted in perfect obedience to His Father and always in fullest fellowship and harmony with Him.

This verse has often been used by false teachers to support their claim that Jesus Christ was not God. They say that because He could not do anything of His own self, He was therefore just a man. But the verse actually proves the very opposite. Men have free will to do what they will, things that may please God or not. But because of who He was, the Lord Jesus could not so act. It was not a matter of being a physical impossibility, but a moral impossibility. He had the physical power to do all things, but He could not do anything that was wrong: and it would have been wrong for Him to have done anything that was not the will of God the Father for Him. This statement sets the Lord Jesus apart from every other person who ever lived.

The Lord Jesus listened to His Father constantly; these promptings governed how He thought, taught, and conducted Himself. The word "judge" in this verse does not have the sense of deciding on legal matters, but of deciding what was proper for Him to do and to say. Because Christ had no selfish motives, He would always decide matters fairly and impartially. His one ambition was to please His Father and to do His will. Our opinions and teachings are affected by what we want to do and to believe—but not so with the Son of God.

"The Father Himself has testified of Me" (vv. 31-47)

In the remaining verses of this chapter, the Lord Jesus Christ described the various witnesses to His deity. There was the witness of John the Baptist (vv. 32-35); the witness of His works (v. 36); the witness of the Father (vv. 37-38); and the witness of the Old Testament Scriptures (vv. 39-47).

Jesus Speaks of Those Who Testified of His Deity

First, Jesus made a general statement on the subject of bearing testimony. He said, "If I bear witness of Myself, My witness is not true." The witness of a single person was not considered sufficient evidence in a court of law. God's divine decree was that two or three witnesses were required to establish testimony and to make it possible for a valid judgment to be formed. Jesus therefore cited not two or three witnesses to His deity, but five: the Father, John the Baptist, His miracles, the Old Testament Scriptures, and Moses.

The Father

There is a question as to whom verse 32 refers to. Some believe that the word "another" describes John the Baptist and that this verse is linked with the three that follow. Others believe that Jesus was speaking here about the witness the Holy Spirit bears concerning Him. We believe that He was referring to the witness of the Father.

John the Baptist

Having introduced the greatest of all witnesses, His Father, the Lord then referenced the testimony of *John*. He reminded the unbelieving Jews in verse 33 that they sent men to John to hear what he had to say, and that John's testimony was all about Him. Instead of pointing people to himself, he pointed them to Christ. John bore witness to the One who is the truth.

Jesus reminded His listeners in verse 34 that His claim to be equal with God was not based simply on human testimony. If that was all He had, then His case would indeed be a weak one. However, He introduced the testimony of John the Baptist because he was a man sent from God and who testified that Jesus of Nazareth was indeed the Messiah. If the Jews had, as a nation, believed John's message, it would have led them to national spiritual salvation, just as it had for individuals who chose to follow Christ. Jesus' words, "But I say these things that you may be saved," give us a wonderful view of His loving and tender heart. He spoke to those who hated Him and who would soon be seeking in every possible way to take His life. But he did not hate *them*. He could only love them.

Here in verse 35 Christ pays tribute to John the Baptist as "the burning and shining lamp." This meant that he was a very zealous man, one who had a ministry that enlightened others, and one who was consumed in the process of pointing people to Jesus. At first, the Jewish people had flocked to John; he was something of a novelty, and they went out to listen to him. For a season they accepted him as a popular religious teacher. Why then, after accepting John so warmly, would they not accept the One of whom John preached? Jesus paid high tribute to John. May each of us who loves the Lord Jesus desire that we, too, be flames of fire for Him, burning ourselves out as we bring light to the world.

The Miracles

The testimony of John was not Christ's greatest proof of His deity (v. 36). The *miracles* He did bore witness of Him; they authenticated the fact that He had been truly sent by God. Miracles in themselves are not a proof of deity. In the Bible, we read of men who were given the power to perform miracles, and we even read of evil beings with the power to do supernatural wonders. But Christ's miracles were different from all others. He had the power *in Himself* to do these mighty works, whereas others were *given* the power. Other men have performed miracles, but they could not confer the power to perform miracles on others. Jesus not only performed miracles Himself, but He gave His apostles the authority to do likewise. What's more, the mighty works that Christ performed were the very ones prophesied in the Old Testament and attributed to the Messiah. Finally, His miracles were unique in character, scope, and number.

The Father (again)

Again the Lord spoke of the witness *the Father* had borne to Him (v. 37). Perhaps this referred to the time when Jesus was baptized. Then the voice of God the Father was heard from heaven stating that Jesus was His beloved Son, in whom He was well pleased. But it should be added that in the life, ministry, and miracles of Christ, the Father also bore witness to the fact that He was the very Son of God.

The Scriptures

Although the Jews had the Old Testament Scriptures, they were deaf to God's voice in that they did not allow God to speak to them through those writings. Their hearts were hardened, and their ears were dull of hearing. And although the incarnate Son of God stood right before them, Jesus could truly say they had not seen God's form because to believe is to see, and they did not believe in the One whom God had sent. In a very real way, those who believed on Christ saw the form of God. Unbelievers merely looked upon Him as another man like themselves.

The Scriptures witnessed of Christ. The first part of verse 39 may be understood in two ways: Jesus was either *telling* the Jews to search the Scriptures, or He was simply *stating the fact* that because they possessed the Scriptures, they thought they had eternal life. Either interpretation of the verse is possible, but we believe the latter is more likely. They did not realize that the Old Testament Scriptures telling of the coming Messiah were actually telling about this man Jesus. It is terrible to think that people with the Scriptures in their hands could be so blind. But it was even more inexcusable that after Christ spoke to them in this way, they still refused to accept Him. Notice the latter part of this verse carefully. "These are they which testify of Me." This simply means that the main subject of the Old Testament Scriptures was the coming of Christ. To miss that is to miss the most important part of it.

The Jews were not willing to come to Christ that they might have life. Here we have the real reason why people do not accept the Savior. It is not because they cannot understand the gospel, or find it impossible to believe in Jesus. There is nothing about Him that makes it impossible for them to trust Him. The real fault lies in man's own will. He loves his sins more than he loves Jesus Christ. He does not want to give up his wicked ways.

In condemning the Jews for their failure to receive Him, the Lord did not want them to think that He was hurt because they had not given Him honor (v. 41). He did not come into the world for the purpose of being praised by the men and women of this world. He was not dependent on their praise, but rather sought the praise of His Father. Even if men rejected Him, that did not detract from His glory. Man's failure to receive the Son of God is traced back to its cause. These people did not have the love of God in them—that is, they loved themselves rather than God. If they had loved God, they would have received the One whom God had sent. By their rejection of the Lord Jesus, they showed their utter lack of love for God.

The Lord Jesus came in His Father's name, that is, He came to do His Father's will, to bring glory to His Father, and to obey His Father in all things. If men and women had really loved God, they would have loved the One who sought to please God in all that He did and said.

Jesus predicted in verse 43 that another man would come in his own name and that the Jews would receive him. Although there are several ways of interpreting this verse, Jesus was probably referring here to the antichrist. In a coming day, a self-appointed ruler will rise among the Jewish people and demand to be worshiped as God (2 Thess. 2:8-10). The majority of the Jewish nation will accept this antichrist as their ruler, and as a result they will come under severe judgment from God (Rev. 13:11-18; Matt. 24:15).

Then Jesus gave another reason for the failure of the Jewish people to accept Him: they were more interested in the approval of their fellow men than in God's approval. They were not willing to endure the reproach and suffering which would be heaped upon them if they became His followers. In order to believe on the Lord Jesus, one must desire God's approval more than anyone else's.

Moses

Christ would not need to accuse these Jews to the Father. He could bring many charges against them, but there would be no need for Him to do so because the writings of *Moses* would be sufficient to accuse them (v. 45). The Jews took great pride in the Old Testament Scriptures, and especially in the writings of Moses, but they did not obey those Scriptures, as we shall see in the next verse. Jesus put the writings of Moses on the same level of authority as His own words. If the Jews had believed Moses, they would have believed Jesus also, because Moses wrote concerning His coming. In Deuteronomy 18:15 and 18, Moses predicted the coming of a "Prophet like [him]." Moses told Israel to listen to him and to obey him when he came. In speaking to Moses of this Prophet, God said, "I . . . will put My words in His mouth, and He shall speak to them all that I command Him." That God-appointed Prophet had now come, but the present-day Jews failed to receive Him. Thus Moses would accuse them to the Father because they professed to believe in Moses and yet did not do what Moses commanded. The words "he wrote about Me" are a clear statement by our Lord that the Old Testament Scriptures contain prophecies about Him.

If the Jews would not believe the writings of Moses, it was unlikely that they would believe the sayings of Jesus (v. 47). There is a close connection between the Old Testament and the New. If someone doubts the inspiration of the Old Testament, it is not likely that he will accept the words of Christ as being inspired. If men attack certain portions of the Bible, it will not be long before they cast doubt on the rest of the Book as well.

CHAPTER

8

JESUS FEEDS 5000+ AND TEACHES ON THE BREAD FROM HEAVEN
JOHN 6:1-34

"What are [5 barley loaves and 2 small fish] among so many?" (vv. 1-15)

The expression "after these things" in verse 1 means that a period of time had elapsed since the events in Jerusalem recorded in chapter 5. Just how much time, we do not know. The city of Tiberias was located on the western bank of the Sea of Galilee. The Passover that John mentions (v. 4) would have been the Feast prior to the one when Jesus was crucified, thus this incident occurred just over a year prior to His death.

This narrative is clearly very significant in that it is recorded in each of the four gospels. As to why John chooses to include these two miracles (the feeding of the 5000 and Christ walking on the water) from the many He performed in Galilee, Charles Erdman comments:

> It is because these miracles, with their related discourses, led to a crisis among the followers of Christ, resulting in a marked division and in an open confession of unbelief and faith. Chapter 6 is therefore a proper sequence and a parallel to chapter 5.

Jesus Shows Compassion

Jesus was not annoyed at the crowds. Instead, His first thought was to provide something for them to eat (v. 5)—an act of compassion and love, truly divine characteristics. He asked Philip where bread could be purchased to feed the multitude. Now, whenever Jesus asked a question, it was never to add to His own knowledge, but as a teaching tool. He was going to teach Philip a valuable lesson and test his faith. Jesus knew He would perform a miracle to feed this great crowd. But would Philip confess his helplessness, and Christ's all-sufficiency? Would Philip (or any of the disciples) respond with "We can't feed them, but we believe You can, Lord!"? Was Philip's faith great or small? Well, Philip's faith did not rise to great heights. He made a rapid mental estimate and decided how much money was needed to buy enough bread to provide even a minimal meal for everyone. A denarius was a working man's daily wage.

Jesus Teaches His Disciples

Andrew, Simon Peter's brother, had noticed a boy with five barley loaves and two small fish—but how could such a meager lunch satisfy the hunger of so many? The boy did not have much, but he was willing to put it at Jesus' disposal. The use of the word "men" in verse 10 reveals that the figure of five thousand did not include all the women and children present. Jesus set us an example by giving thanks for the food—how much more should *we* thank God before eating our meals! Next, He enlisted the service of others in distributing the food. By the time that was done, it had been wonderfully multiplied. There was no scarcity; the people had "as much as they wanted." This miracle involved a true act of creation on the part of the Creator of all things.

> **Jesus set us an example by giving thanks for the food—how much more should *we* thank God before eating our meals!**

In verse 12 Jesus set another practical example to His followers by instructing them to collect up the leftovers. Jesus is God, and with God there must be no wasting of His bounties. He does not want us to squander the precious things He has given us. Many Bible critics try to explain away this miracle. The crowd, they say, saw the boy give his lunch to Jesus. This made others realize how selfish they were, so they took out their lunches and shared them around. But twelve baskets of bread wouldn't have been gathered up if each person shared their own food. No, indeed! On the contrary, a mighty miracle had been performed!

Jesus Evades the People's Call to Kingship

We see in verse 14 that the people themselves recognized the miracle. They were so convinced that it was a miracle that they wondered aloud if Jesus could be the Prophet that Moses predicted was to come (Deut. 18:18). As a result of Jesus' miracle, the people wanted to make Him their king—but on their terms, not His. Their idea of a king was someone who would deliver them from the Roman government who occupied their land. They were not interested on being delivered from sin and its penalty. The following day their professed faith in Jesus was to be tested, and found to be not genuine. Of course, Jesus knew the state of their hearts.

"It is I; do not be afraid" (vv. 16-21)

It was now evening. Jesus had gone into the mountain alone. The crowd had been sent home, and the disciples went down to the beach to prepare for their boat trip back across the Sea of Galilee. Now, the Sea of Galilee is subject to very violent storms. Winds sweep down the valley of the River Jordan and raise mountainous waves on the water. It is not safe for small boats to be out on the sea at such a time. The disciples had rowed between three and four miles and were in great danger. Suddenly, they looked up and saw Jesus walking on the water, coming near to them. They were afraid.

Notice how simply the story is told. John relates the most amazing facts but does not use big words to impress us with the greatness of what was taking place. Instead he uses great restraint in setting forth the facts.

> The Lord Jesus is the mighty Creator, the Sustainer of the universe. There is no reason to fear.

Jesus Controls the Sea

The Lord Jesus spoke a wonderful word of comfort in verse 20. "It is I; do not be afraid," He said. The mighty Creator, the Sustainer of the universe, was at hand. There was no reason to fear. He who had made the Sea of Galilee could calm its waters and bring these men safely to shore. The words "It is I" actually read in the original Greek, "I AM." So, for the second time in John's gospel, Jesus appropriated to Himself the name of Jehovah. When the disciples realized it was Jesus, they welcomed Him aboard. As soon as they did this, they found themselves at their destination.

Here another miracle is stated but not explained. They did not have to row any farther; the Lord Jesus brought them to dry land instantly. What a wonderful person He is!

"Do not labor for the food which perishes" (vv. 22-34)

It was now the next day. Multitudes were still in the area northeast of the Sea of Galilee. They had watched the disciples get into the boat the previous evening and knew that Jesus had not gone with them in the only boat that had then been available.

Now, more small boats arrived from Tiberias to where Jesus had fed the multitude. But He could not have departed in one of these, because they had just arrived. Perhaps it was in these small boats that the multitude crossed over to Capernaum, as recorded in verses 24 and 25.

When they arrived, they found Jesus there too. Unable to conceal their curiosity as to how He had got there, they asked Him. He did not answer their question directly because He knew they were only interested in more food. (We do well to remember that Jesus never performed a miracle just for the immediate benefit it spawned; in many respects His miracles were parables in action, as His goal was that the people learn lessons of spiritual truth from them.) They had eaten of the miracle loaves, and their hunger had been satisfied, so Jesus counseled them not to labor for the food which perishes (v. 27). He did not mean that they should not work for their daily living, but that this should not be the supreme goal of their lives.

> Jesus' miracles were parables in action, as His goal was that the people learn lessons of spiritual truth from them.

Satisfying physical hunger is not the most important thing in life. Man consists not only of body, but of spirit and soul as well. We should work for the food which endures to everlasting life—the spiritual food, the teaching, of the Lord Jesus. The value of physical food ends at the grave; the value of the words of the Lord Jesus never ends. Man should make sure that his soul is fed day by day with the Word of God. In saying that God the Father had set His seal on Him, Christ meant that God had sent Him and approved Him. God had endorsed Christ Jesus as One who spoke the truth.

The people now asked Jesus what they ought to do to work the works of God (v. 28). Jesus saw through their hypocrisy. They pretended that they wanted to work for God, yet wanted nothing to do with God's Son. Jesus told them they must first accept the One whom God had sent. So it is today. Many are seeking to earn their way to heaven by good works. The only "good work" a sinner can do is to confess his sins and receive Christ as his Lord and Savior. The Bible teaches that good works do not precede salvation—they follow it.

> **The Bible teaches that good works do not precede salvation—they follow it.**

Jesus Compares Manna to the Bread of Life

We learn from verse 30 how corrupt were the hearts of the people. Just the day before, they had witnessed and experienced Christ's power. Now they asked Him for some miracle that would prove He was the Son of God. Referring to their nation's history, the Jews reminded Jesus of the miracle of the manna in the wilderness. (Manna was a small, round, white substance that God miraculously provided for Israel in the wilderness. They had to gather it from the ground each morning the first six days of every week.) In raising the topic of the manna in the wilderness, they were implying that Jesus had done nothing as wonderful as that. They quoted from Psalm 78:24-25, "He [God] rained down manna for them to eat." The inference was that Jesus was not as great as Moses because He had only multiplied *existing* food, whereas Moses called down food from heaven.

In verse 32 Jesus pointed out that it was not Moses who gave them the manna, but God. Moreover, the manna was not the *spiritual* bread from heaven; the manna *was* literal food, designed for the physical body, but it had no value beyond this life. The Lord Jesus was here speaking about the true, ideal, and genuine bread which God gives out of heaven—bread for the soul, not the body. The words "My Father" were a claim by Christ to deity.

The Lord Jesus did not at this point claim to be the bread of God. He simply said the bread of God was that bread which came down out of heaven and which was life-giving. He was showing the superiority of the bread of God to the manna in the wilderness. The manna did not give life, it only sustained existing physical life. And it was not intended for the whole world, only for the nation of Israel. The Jews still did not realize that Jesus was speaking about Himself as the true bread, and so they asked Him for it. But they were still thinking in terms of literal bread; there was no real faith in their hearts.

CHAPTER

9

JESUS IS THE BREAD OF LIFE
JOHN 6:35-59

"I am the bread of life" (vv. 35-40)

In verse 35 the Lord Jesus states the truth simply and clearly: He is the bread of life. Those who come to Him find enough in Him to satisfy their spiritual hunger forever. Those who believe in Him find their thirst forever quenched. You will notice the words "I am" in this verse and recognize Christ was claiming equality with Jehovah again. It would be folly for a sinful man to utter such words as these. No mere man can satisfy his own spiritual hunger or thirst, to say nothing of satisfying the spiritual appetite of the whole world.

> Those who come to Christ find enough in Him to satisfy their spiritual hunger forever.

We saw in verse 30 that the unbelieving Jews had asked the Lord for a sign so they might see and believe. Yet they had seen *Him*—the greatest sign of all—and did not believe. If the Son of God could stand before them in perfect manhood and not be "recognized" by them, it was doubtful that *any* sign would convince them.

God's Purposes Will Be Fulfilled

The Lord was not discouraged by the unbelief of the Jews. He knew that all the Father's purposes and plans would be fulfilled. Even if the Jews to whom He was speaking would not accept Him, all those chosen by God would come to Him. As A. W. Pink puts it, "The realization of the invincibility of the eternal counsels of God gives a calmness, a poise, a courage, a perseverance which nothing else can."

Verse 37 is very important because it teaches two vital truths. First, God has given certain ones to His Son, and all those whom He has given will be saved. Second, man is a responsible creature. To be saved, a person must come to Christ and receive Him by faith. God does choose some people to be saved, but He does not choose some to be damned. If anyone is saved, it is due to the grace of God, since no one can say they deserve salvation. But if anyone perishes forever, it is his own fault. We are all condemned by our own sinfulness and wickedness. If we all went to hell, we would be receiving only what we deserve. In grace, God stoops down and saves individual people out of the great mass of humanity. Does He have the right to do this? He certainly does. God can do whatever He wants to do and no one can deny Him this right. Moreover, God cannot do anything wrong or unjust.

God has elected certain persons to be saved, but man is responsible to receive and believe Christ. God makes a universal offer that if a person will believe in the Lord Jesus Christ, he or she will be saved. God does not save people against their will. We must come to Him in repentance and faith—then God will save us. No one who comes to God through Christ will be cast out. The human mind cannot reconcile these two teachings. However, we should believe them even if we cannot understand them. They are both biblical teachings, and they are clearly stated in this verse.

Jesus Fulfills God's Will

Since all God's plans would eventually be fulfilled with regard to the salvation of those who were given to Him, the Lord Jesus would personally undertake to make it happen, as His mission was to do the will of God. Coming into the world, He was the obedient Son of God. He voluntarily took the place of a servant in order to carry out His Father's will; His own will agreed perfectly with God's will.

The will of the Father was that everyone who was given to Christ would be saved and kept until the resurrection of the just, at which point they would be raised and taken home to heaven (v. 39). The words "nothing" and "it" refer to believers, but not to individual believers. They refer to the entire body of Christians who would be saved down through the years. The Lord Jesus was responsible to see that not one member of the body would be lost; the whole body will be raised up at the last day. "The last day," as far as *Christians* are concerned, refers to the day when Christ will come in the air, when believers will be caught up to meet Him and to be forever with Him. To the *Jews,* it meant the coming of Messiah in glory.

Jesus now went on in verse 40 to explain how a person becomes a member of the family of the redeemed. God's will is that everyone who "sees the Son" and believes in Him should have everlasting life. To see the Son means to see Him with the eyes of faith. One must perceive, recognize, that Jesus Christ is the Son of God and the promised Redeemer. Then, too, he must by a conscious act of faith take Jesus Christ as his own Lord and Savior. Everyone who does this receives everlasting life as a present possession and the assurance that they will be raised at the last day.

"He who believes in Me has everlasting life" (vv. 41-59)

These Jewish people were quite unprepared to accept Jesus as the Christ, and they showed this by complaining about Him. He had claimed to be the bread of God that had come down from heaven, and they realized this was a significant claim. To come down from heaven, one could not be a mere man, or even a great prophet. And so they complained at Him because they were not willing to believe what He said. They assumed that Jesus was the son of Joseph. Of course, they were wrong. Jesus was born of the Virgin Mary and conceived of the Holy Spirit. Their failure to believe in the virgin birth led to their darkness and unbelief. So it is today. Those who refuse to believe that Jesus is the Son of God who came into the world through the womb of the virgin find themselves compelled to deny all the great truths concerning the person and work of Christ.

The more the Jews rejected the testimony of the Lord Jesus, the more difficult His teachings became to them. Someone put the principle this way: "Light rejected is light denied." If the Lord Jesus told them simple things and they would not believe, they would certainly be thoroughly ignorant of any deeper truths He might expound.

The Father Draws People

Man in himself is utterly hopeless and helpless. He does not even have the strength to come to Jesus by himself (v. 44). Unless the Father first begins to work in a person's heart and life, that person will never realize his terrible guilt and his need of a Savior. Many people have difficulty with this verse. They suppose it teaches that someone may desire to be saved and yet might find it impossible. This is not so. The verse teaches in the strongest possible way that God is the One who first acts in our lives to win us to Himself. We have the choice of embracing the Lord Jesus or refusing Him. But we would never have had the desire in the first place if God had not spoken to our hearts. Again Jesus added the promise that He will raise up every true believer at the last day. As we have seen before, this refers to Christ's coming for His saints when the dead will be raised and those still alive will be changed. It is a resurrection of believers only.

Having stated strongly that no one can come to Him unless the Father draws him, Jesus goes on in verse 45 to explain how the Father does that. First, He quotes from Isaiah 54:13. "And they shall all be taught by God." God speaks to the hearts of men and women, boys and girls, through what He has revealed in His written Word about Himself, His Son, mankind, and His plan for the ages. Then, the person's own will is involved. Those who respond to the teaching of Scripture are the ones who come to Christ. Here again the two great truths of God's sovereignty and man's free will are placed side by side, like railroad tracks. They show that salvation has a divine side and a human side. When Jesus said, "It is written in the prophets," He probably meant Isaiah in particular, though the thought He expressed here permeates throughout all the books of the Old Testament prophets. By the teaching of God's Word and God's Spirit, people are drawn to God.

The fact that people are taught by God does not mean that they have seen Him (v. 46). Jesus Christ, having come from God, is the only One who has seen Him. All those who are taught by God are taught about Christ, because God's teaching has Christ Himself as its grand subject.

One of the clearest and briefest statements in the whole Bible about the way of salvation is found in John 6:47. Notice Jesus introduced these words with His familiar phrase, "Most assuredly." This is one of many New Testament verses which teach that salvation is not by works, law-keeping, church membership, or obeying the Golden Rule, but simply by believing in faith and full dependence in the Lord Jesus Christ.

Jesus Feeds People

In verse 48 Jesus states that *He* is the bread of life of which He had been speaking. The "bread of life" means, of course, the source of life to those who take it in. The Jews had previously referenced the manna in the wilderness and challenged Jesus to produce some food as wonderful as that. He reminded them that their fathers had eaten the manna and were now dead. In other words, the manna was for this life only. It had no power to impart eternal life to those who ate it.

In contrast to the manna, the Lord Jesus spoke of Himself as the bread which comes down from heaven (v. 50). If anyone ate of this bread, he would not die. This did not mean that he wouldn't die physically, but that he would never die spiritually. Even if he did die physically, his body would be raised at the last day, and he would spend eternity with the Lord.

In this and in the following verses, Jesus spoke repeatedly of being eaten. What did He mean? Did He mean we must eat of Him in a physical, literal way? Obviously, that idea is impossible and repulsive. Some think, however, that we must eat of Him in the communion service; that in some miraculous way, the bread and wine are changed into Christ's body and blood, and that in order to be saved we must partake of those emblems. But this is not what Jesus said. The context makes it quite clear that to *eat His flesh* means to believe in Him, to *appropriate* Him by faith as our Savior. "He must be taken into every sphere and experience of life. His words and will must be assimilated, and become part of our very being" (Erdman).

Jesus is the living bread. He not only lives in Himself, but is life-giving. Those who eat of this bread will live forever. But how? How can Jesus give eternal life to guilty sinners? The answer is found in the latter part of this verse. "The bread that I shall give is My flesh, which I shall give for the life of the world." Here the Lord Jesus was pointing forward to His death on the cross, where He would suffer greatly at the hands of both God and man, and where His blood would be poured out, as it were, as a sacrifice for sins. He would die as a Substitute, paying the penalty for sin demanded by a holy God. And why? "For the life of the world." This does not mean that the whole world will be saved, but that the work of Christ at Calvary would be sufficient in its value to save the whole world if all came to Jesus.

> To "eat Christ's flesh" means to believe in Him, to *appropriate* him by faith as our Savior.

The Jews were still thinking in terms of literal bread and flesh (v. 52). They did not realize that Jesus was using physical things to teach spiritual truths. And so they asked among themselves how a mere man could possibly give his flesh to be eaten by others. Of course, Jesus knew exactly what they were thinking and saying. He warned them solemnly that if they did not eat His flesh and drink His blood, they would have no life in them. Compare verse 54 with verse 47. It proves that to eat His flesh and to drink His blood means to believe on Him. In verse 47, we read that "he who *believes* in Me has everlasting life." In verse 54, we learn that those who *eat* His flesh and *drink* His blood have eternal life. Now, things equal to the same thing are equal to each other. To eat His flesh and to drink His blood is to believe in Him. All who believe in Him will be raised up at the last day. This refers, of course, to the bodies of those who have died trusting in the Lord Jesus.

The flesh of the Lord Jesus is true food, and His blood is true drink. This is in contrast to the food and drink of this world, which is only of temporary value. The value of the death of the Lord Jesus is never-ending. Those who partake of Him by faith receive life that goes on eternally. When we eat literal food, we take it into our very being; and it becomes a part of us. When we receive the Lord Jesus, we are taking Him into our lives; His life becomes our life, and He sustains us forevermore.

In verse 57 the Lord Jesus gave another illustration of the close bond that existed between Himself and His people. The illustration was His own connection with God the Father. The Father had sent the Lord Jesus into the world. As a man here in the world, the Lord Jesus lived by the Father, that is, because of the Father or by reason of the Father. His life was lived in closest union and harmony with God the Father. God was the center and circumference of His life. His purpose was to be occupied with God the Father. He was here as a man in the world, and the world did not realize that He was God manifest in the flesh. Although He was misunderstood by the world, yet He and His Father were one. They lived in the closest intimacy. That is exactly the way it is with those who are believers in the Lord Jesus. They are here in the world, misunderstood by the world, and hated and persecuted. But because they have put their faith and trust in the Lord Jesus, they live by reason of Him. Their lives are closely bound up with His life, and this life will endure forever.

Verse 58 seems to be a summary of all that the Lord has said in the previous verses. He is the bread which came down from heaven. He is superior to the manna which the fathers ate in the wilderness. That bread was only of temporary value. It was only for this life. But Christ is the bread of God who gives eternal life to all who appropriate Him by faith.

CHAPTER

10

JESUS' TEACHING CREATES CONTROVERSY
JOHN 6:60–7:24

"Some of you . . .do not believe" (6:60-65)

You will remember that the crowd had followed the Lord Jesus and the Twelve to Capernaum from the northeast side of the Sea of Galilee. Apparently, the multitude (or, representatives of them) had found Jesus in the synagogue, and it was there that He delivered His discourse on the bread of life to them. (A synagogue is a Jewish religious meeting place. It is not the same as the temple, where the sacrifices were offered.) From this point on, Jesus addresses His disciples, not the Jews with whom He had been interacting in the synagogue (v. 60).

By this time in His public ministry, the Lord Jesus had many disciples ("learners") in addition to the Twelve. Anyone who followed Him and professed to accept His teachings was termed a disciple. However, they were not all genuine believers. (We should remember, however, that the term *disciples* often refers to the Twelve in the gospel accounts.) This passage signals a crisis of faith for Christ's followers, for we read that some of those who professed to be His disciples said, "This is a hard saying." They meant that His teaching offended them (in verses 53-58 in particular). It was not so much that they did not understand what He said, but that it was distasteful to them—they could not "stomach" it. They said, "Who can understand it?" meaning, "Who can stand to listen to such offensive doctrine?"

Jesus knew exactly what they were saying, and He confronted them. "Does this offend you?" He asked. He would soon be revealing things that would be harder for them to receive than what He had just told them. For instance, having said He had come down from heaven (v. 38), what would they think if they witnessed Him returning to heaven (v. 62)? Westcott has the following perspective on this verse: "The Passion, the Resurrection, the Ascension, were steps in the progress of the 'ascending up' through suffering, which is the great offense of the Gospel." Thus it is likely, given Christ's heavy use of metaphoric language in this section, that He was referring to His crucifixion here as well as His literal ascension.

These professing disciples had been thinking in terms of Christ's literal flesh, but in verse 63 He told them that eternal life was not gained by eating flesh, but by the work of the Holy Spirit of God. Flesh cannot give life; only the Spirit can do this. They had taken His words literally and had not realized that they were to be understood spiritually. The words that Jesus spoke were spirit and life—that is, eating His flesh and drinking His blood equate to metaphors—word pictures—for believing in Him, accepting the message, and thereby gaining eternal life.

The difficulty lay not so much in their *inability* to believe as in their *unwillingness* to believe. Christ knew from the beginning of His earthly ministry that some of His professed followers would not believe on Him, and that one of the chosen Twelve would go so far as to betray Him. Of course, as the eternal Son, He knew all this from eternity, but here it probably means that He was aware of it from the very beginning of His ministry on earth.

Christ's statement in verse 65 speaks to human pride, for man thinks he can earn or merit salvation. The Lord Jesus told these people that even the power to come to Him can only be given by God the Father.

"Lord . . . You have the words of eternal life" (6:66-71)

These sayings of the Lord Jesus proved so distasteful to many who had followed Him that they now left Him. They were no longer willing to associate with Him. As mentioned previously, these people were never true believers in the first place. They followed Jesus for various reasons, but not out of genuine love for Him or appreciation for who He was. At this point, Jesus turned to the twelve disciples and challenged them with the question as to whether they, too, would leave Him (v. 67). Peter said in effect, "Lord, how could we leave You? You teach the doctrines which lead to eternal life. If we leave You, there is no one else to whom we could go. To leave You would be to seal our doom." Speaking for the Twelve, Peter further said that they had believed and had come to know that the Lord Jesus was the Holy One of God. Notice again the order of the words "believe . . . know." After putting their faith in Christ, they had come to know that He was indeed all He claimed to be.

Peter said "we," meaning all twelve of the disciples, but Jesus corrected him. One in the company did not share Peter's views concerning Him. Jesus knew that Judas would betray Him. Here again John presents testimony of Christ's omniscience, and therefore of His deity.

"My time has not yet come" (7:1-9)

There was a lapse of some months between the events of chapters 6 and 7. Jesus remained in Galilee; He chose not to go to Judea because the Jews there sought to kill Him. The Jews referred to in verse 1 were the leaders, or rulers. They hated the Lord Jesus bitterly, and they sought opportunities to destroy Him.

The Feast of Tabernacles mentioned in verse 2 was one of the important events in the Jewish calendar. It came at harvest and celebrated the time in the nation's history when the Israelites lived in temporary shelters (booths) after they came out of Egypt. It was a joyful, festive occasion, and looked forward to a coming day when the saved Jewish nation would dwell in the land of Israel, and when the Messiah would reign in peace and prosperity.

Jesus' brothers mentioned in verse 3 may have been sons born to Mary after the birth of Jesus, or they may have been cousins or other distant relatives. But no matter how close their relationship to Jesus was, they were not automatically believers in His true identity as the Christ. The advice they give Jesus implies they thought He was looking for publicity. "Now's your big chance," they said in effect. "You should go to Jerusalem for the feast. If You are doing these miracles to prove You are the Messiah, why don't You offer these proofs where they will really count, namely, in Judea?" They had no sincere desire to see Him glorified. They did not really believe Him to be the Messiah. Neither were they willing to trust themselves to Him. It must have been especially bitter for the Lord Jesus to have His own family doubt His words and His works. Yet how often it is, that those who are faithful to God find their bitterest opposition from those who are nearest and dearest to them!

The Lord's life was ordered from beginning to end (v. 6). Each day and every movement was in accordance with a pre-arranged schedule. The time for manifesting Himself openly to the world had not yet come. He knew exactly what lay before Him, and it was not God's will that He should go to Jerusalem at this time to present Himself publicly. They lived according to their own desires; they had no desire to obey God. They could make their own plans and travel as they pleased, because they were only intent on doing what *they* wanted. The world could not hate the brothers of Jesus because they belonged to the world. They sided with the world against Jesus. Their whole lives were in harmony with the world. "The world" here refers to the system which man has built up and in which there is no room for God or His Christ, the world of culture, art, education, and religion. Judea epitomized particularly the religious world, and it was the rulers of the Jews who hated Christ the most.

The world hated Christ because He testified that its works were evil. It is a sad commentary on man's depraved nature that when a sinless man came into the world, the world sought to kill Him. The perfection of Christ's life showed the imperfection of everyone else's. Man resented this exposure of himself and instead of repenting and crying to God for mercy, he sought to destroy the One who revealed his sin.

Not to be hated by the world—to be loved and flattered and caressed by the world—is one of the most terrible positions in which a Christian can find himself. The absence of the world's hate proves that we do not testify against it that its works are evil. The warmth of the world's love proves that we are of its own. Friendship with the world is enmity with God. Whoever wants to be a friend of the world is the enemy of God (John 7:7; 15:19; James 4:4).

> Whoever wants to be a friend of the world is the enemy of God.

Verse 8 tells us that the Lord told His brothers to go up to the feast. Notice the sad irony here. These men pretended to be religious. They were going to keep the Feast of Tabernacles. Yet the Christ of God was standing in their midst, and they had no real love for Him. Man loves religious rituals because he can observe them without any real heart interest. But bring him face to face with the person of Christ and he is ill at ease. The Lord Jesus said He would not go up to the feast as yet because His time had not yet fully come. He did not mean He would not go there at all, but that He would not go with His brethren and present Himself publicly. It was not the time for that. When He went, He would go quietly and with a minimum of publicity. So He remained in Galilee after His brethren had left for Jerusalem.

"There was much complaining among the people concerning Him" (7:10-24)

Sometime later, Jesus did make a quiet trip there. As a devout Jew, He desired to attend the feast. The Jews who sought Him at the feast were no doubt the rulers who sought to kill Him. Verse 12 makes it clear that the Lord was creating quite a stir among the people. More and more, the miracles He performed were compelling people to make up their minds as to who He really was. There was an undercurrent of conversation at the feast as to whether He was genuine or a false prophet. Some said He was a good man. Others said He deceived the people. But the opposition of the rulers against Jesus had become so intense that no one dared to speak openly in favor of Him.

The Feast of Tabernacles lasted for several days, and in verse 14 we see a change: half way through it, the Lord went up to the porch of the temple where the people were allowed to gather and be taught. Those who heard Him were amazed—His knowledge of the Scriptures, the breadth of His learning, and His ability to teach garnered their attention. Jesus had never been to any of the great schools, so how could He know so much? Jesus refused to take any credit for Himself; He simply sought to glorify His Father. He answered that His teaching was not His own, but came from the One who sent Him. Whatever the Lord Jesus spoke and whatever He taught were the things that His Father told Him to speak and to teach. He never acted independently of the Father.

There is a wonderful promise in verse 17 for everyone earnestly seeking truth. If a man is sincere, if he truly wants to know what is truth, God will reveal it to him. Anyone who speaks from himself, that is, according to his own will, seeks his own glory. But it was not so with the Lord Jesus. He sought the glory of the Father who had sent Him. Because His motives were absolutely pure, His message was absolutely true. There was no unrighteousness in Him. The Lord was the only One of whom such words could be spoken. Every other teacher has had some selfishness mixed in his service. It should be the ambition of every servant of the Lord to glorify God rather than self.

In verse 19 Christ then made a direct accusation against the Jews. They gloried in the fact that they possessed the Law which God gave them through Moses, but they forgot there was no virtue in merely possessing it. The Law demanded obedience to its commands. Although they gloried in the Law, it was plain they weren't keeping it as they were planning to break one of its chief standards by taking a life—*His!* They were plotting to kill the Lord Jesus. The Jews felt the sharp edge of Jesus' accusation, but rather than admit He was right, they began to abuse Him, accusing Him of being demon-possessed.

> **It should be the ambition of every servant of the Lord to glorify God rather than self.**

In verses 21 through 24 Jesus answered their question. He referred to the healing of the lame man at the pool of Bethesda. It was this miracle that had stirred the hatred of the Jewish leaders against Him, and it was at this point that they began their vicious plot to kill Him. They were shocked He should do such a thing on the Sabbath day. He reasoned with them: The law of Moses commanded that a male child should be circumcised eight days after birth. If the eighth day fell on the Sabbath, the Jews did not consider it wrong to circumcise a baby boy. They conceded that it was a work of necessity, and as such was permissible. Now, if they routinely circumcised a child on the Sabbath day, why should they find fault with Jesus for making a man perfectly well on the Sabbath day? If the Law allowed for a work of necessity, would it not also allow for a work of mercy?

The trouble with the Jews was that they judged things according to outward appearances and not according to inward reality. Their judgment was not righteous. Works that seemed perfectly legitimate when performed by them seemed wrong when performed by Him. Human nature always tends to judge according to sight rather than according to reality. The Lord had not broken the Law; it was they who were breaking it by their senseless hatred of Him.

CHAPTER

11

JESUS IS THE LIGHT OF THE WORLD
JOHN 7:25–8:20

"Is this not He whom they seek to kill?" (7:25-31)

We learn from John 7:25 that, by this time, it had become well known in Jerusalem that the Jewish leaders were plotting against Christ. Here, some of the common people asked if this was not the One whom their rulers were pursuing. They could not understand why Jesus was being allowed to speak so openly and fearlessly. If the rulers hated Him as much as the people had been led to believe, why did they allow Him to continue? Is it possible that they had come to find out that He was really the Messiah after all?

The people who did not believe Jesus to be the Messiah thought they knew where He came from—Nazareth. They knew His mother (Mary) and supposed that Joseph was His father. It was commonly believed by the Jews that when Messiah came, He would come suddenly and mysteriously. They had no idea that He would be born and grow up in the same way all human beings do. That is why they said here in verse 27, "When the Christ comes, no one knows where He is from."

At this point, Jesus cried out to the people who had gathered and were listening to the conversation (v. 28). They did indeed know Him, He said, and they knew where He came from. He was saying, of course, that they knew Him simply as a man, as Jesus of Nazareth. But they would not believe He was also God. They should have realized that He did not come of Himself but had been sent from God the Father, of whom these people were ignorant. Thus Jesus was making a direct claim to equality with God. He had been sent into the world by the true God, and *this* God they did not know. But *He* knew Him. He dwelt with God from all eternity and was equal in all respects with God the Father. In the expression "He has sent Me," the Lord Jesus stated in the clearest possible way that He was the Christ of God, the Anointed One, whom God had sent into the world to accomplish the work of redemption.

From verse 30 it is clear that the Jews understood He was claiming to be the Messiah. They considered this to be blasphemy and tried to arrest Him. But they could not lay their hands on Him because the hour had not yet come in God's plan for Him to die.

Actually, many of the people did place their faith in Christ. We would like to think that their belief was genuine. Their reasoning was this: What more could Jesus do to prove He was the Messiah? Would the Messiah do more numerous or more wonderful miracles than Jesus had done? Obviously they believed the miracles of Jesus *did* authenticate His claim to be the real Messiah.

"You will seek Me and not find Me" (7:32-36)

As the Pharisees moved in and out among the people, they heard this undercurrent of conversation. The people were murmuring about Jesus, not in the sense of complaining against Him, but secretly revealing their admiration for Him. The Pharisees feared this might become a great movement to accept Jesus, so they sent officers again to arrest Him. The words of verses 33 and 34 were undoubtedly spoken to these officers as well as to the Pharisees and to the people in general.

The Lord reminded them He would only be with them (His people, Israel) for a little while, and then He would return to His Father. This only made the Pharisees angrier. In a coming day, Jesus said, the Pharisees would seek Him and would not be able to find Him. He would have gone back to heaven, and because of their unbelief and wickedness, they would not be able to meet Him there. The words of this verse are especially solemn. There is such a thing as a "window of opportunity." People might have the chance to be saved today; if they reject it, they might never have the chance again. But the Jews failed to understand the meaning of the Lord's words (v. 36)

"Come to Me and drink" (7:37-39)

In this section we come to the last day of the Feast of Tabernacles. The Jewish people had gone through this religious observance, and yet their hearts were not satisfied because they no longer truly understood the deep meaning of the feast. Just before they left for home, Jesus stood and cried out to them. He invited them to come to Him for spiritual satisfaction. Pay particular attention to the words. His invitation was extended to "anyone." His was a universal gospel. Anyone could be saved if he would simply come to Christ. But notice the condition. The Scripture says, "If anyone thirsts . . ." "Thirst" here, of course, speaks of spiritual need. Unless a man knows he is a sinner, he will not recognize his need to be saved. Unless he realizes he is lost, he will not desire to be found. Unless a man is conscious of a great spiritual lack in his life, he will not want to go to the Lord to have that need supplied. Jesus Christ invited the thirsting soul to come to Him—not to the church, the preacher, the waters of baptism, or to the communion table. "Come to Me," He said. "Come to Me and *drink*." To "drink" means to appropriate Christ for oneself—to entrust oneself to Him and embrace Him as Savior and Lord.

Verse 38 proves that to come to Christ and "drink" is the same as to *believe* in Him. All who believe in Him will have their own spiritual needs supplied and will receive rivers of blessing enough to flow out to others.

> Every true believer in the Lord Jesus Christ has been permanently indwelt by the Holy Spirit.

It is clearly stated that "living water" refers to the Holy Spirit. Verse 39 is important because it teaches that all who receive the Lord Jesus Christ also receive the Spirit of God. At the time the Lord Jesus spoke, the Holy Spirit had not been given. It was not until after Jesus went back to heaven and was glorified there that the Holy Spirit descended (on the day of Pentecost). From that moment on, every true believer in the Lord Jesus Christ has been permanently indwelt by the Holy Spirit.

"No man ever spoke like this Man!" (7:40-53)

Some of those who listened were now convinced that the Lord Jesus was the Prophet of whom Moses spoke in Deuteronomy 18:15 and 18. Some were even willing to acknowledge that Jesus was the Messiah. But others thought this was impossible. They believed that Jesus came from Nazareth in Galilee, and there was no prophecy in the Old Testament indicating the Messiah would come out of Galilee. The Jews were right in that the Messiah would come from Bethlehem (as predicted in Micah 5:2) and that He would be a descendant of King David. Had they taken the trouble to inquire, they would have found that Jesus was both born in Bethlehem *and* descended directly from David. Because of these differing opinions and the general ignorance, there was a division among the people because of Christ. It is still the same. Men and women are divided on the subject of Jesus Christ. Some say He was simply a man like the rest of us. Others are willing to admit that He was the greatest man who ever lived. But those who believe the Word of God know that the Lord Jesus Christ is God over all, blessed forever.

Efforts were still being made to arrest Jesus, but no one succeeded in taking Him (v. 44). As long as a person is walking in the will of God, no power on earth can hinder him. As someone has said, "We are immortal until our work is done." The Lord Jesus' time had not yet come, and so men were unable to harm Him. We read in verse 32 that the Pharisees and the chief priests had sent officers to arrest Jesus. In verse 45 the officers had returned without Him. The leaders were annoyed and asked the officers why they hadn't brought Him. The officers were compelled to speak well of Christ: "No man ever spoke like this Man!" they said. They had never heard anyone speak with such authority, wisdom, and grace. In an effort to intimidate the officers, the Pharisees accused them of being deceived by Jesus. They reminded them that none of the rulers of the Jewish nation recognized Him as the Christ. What a terrible argument this was! It was to their shame that leading men in the Jewish nation had failed to recognize the Messiah. These Pharisees were not only unwilling to believe in Jesus Christ themselves, but did not want others to believe in Him either. So it is today. Many who do not want to be saved themselves do everything in their power to prevent their relatives and friends from being saved as well.

After attacking the officers, the Pharisees described the mass of the Jewish people as ignorant and cursed (v. 49). They reasoned that if the common people knew anything at all about the Scriptures, they would know that Jesus was not the Messiah. They could not have been more wrong. At this point, Nicodemus spoke up. Apparently, he had at some point expressed saving faith in Christ. Here he stepped forward among the rulers of the

Jews to say a word for his Lord. He claimed they had not given Jesus a fair chance. Jewish law did not condemn a man before it heard his case, yet this was what the Jewish leaders were doing. Were they afraid of the facts? Now the rulers turned on Nicodemus, one of their own company, and asked with a sneer if he was also a follower of Jesus, like the men from Galilee. Did he not know that the Old Testament never spoke of a prophet as coming out of Galilee? In this they showed their own ignorance, for Jonah came from Galilee (2 Kings 14:25).

The Feast of Tabernacles was now over. The men returned to their own homes. Some had met Christ face to face and had trusted in Him. But the vast majority had rejected Him, and the leaders of the Jewish people were more determined than ever to do away with Him. They considered Him a threat to their religion and their way of life.

"Woman, where are those accusers of yours?" (8:1-11)

The first verse of chapter 8 is closely linked with the last verse of the previous chapter. The connection is better seen by putting the two verses together as follows—"And everyone went to his own house. But Jesus went to the Mount of Olives." Jesus had not exaggerated when He said, "Foxes have holes and the birds of the air have nests, but the Son of Man has nowhere to lay His head" (Luke 9:58). The Mount of Olives was not far from the temple. In the morning the Lord walked back down the side of Olivet, crossed the Kidron valley and so on, back to the city, where the temple was located. A great multitude of people came to Him, and He sat down and began to instruct them again.

Before we review these verses we should mentioned that the passage of John 7:53–8:11 does not appear in all the ancient manuscripts of the Bible. There is some question as to whether these verses form a part of the original text. The author of this course believes it is appropriate to accept them as part of the inspired text because everything taught here is in perfect agreement with the rest of the Bible.

In verse 3 we read that the scribes (a group of men who copied and taught the Scriptures) and the Pharisees tried to trap Jesus so they would have some charge to bring against Him. They had caught a woman in the very act of adultery, and they brought her and made her stand in the middle of the crowd, probably facing Jesus. The accusation against the woman was no doubt true. Verse 5 records the words that the accusers used to try to trap Jesus. They wanted Him to contradict the sayings of Moses. If they could succeed in doing that, then they could turn the common people against Him. They reminded Jesus that Moses commanded a person taken in the act of adultery should be stoned to death. For their own wicked purposes, the Pharisees hoped Jesus would disagree, and so they asked Him what He had to say on the subject. As someone has said, "It comforts and quiets the depraved heart of man if he can only find a person worse than himself: he thinks the greater sin of another excuses himself; and while accusing and vehemently blaming another, he forgets his own evil. He thus rejoices in iniquity."

They had no real charge against the Lord Jesus and were trying to manufacture one (v. 6). If He judged that the woman should go free, He would be opposing the Law, and they would accuse Him of being unjust. If He condemned the woman to death, then they could say He was not merciful. What the Lord did, though, was to stoop down and write with His finger on the ground. Dissatisfied, the Jews insisted He respond in some way. Verse 7 records His masterful reply, that the penalty of the Law be carried out, but that it be done by those who had committed no sin. Thus the Lord upheld the Law and at the same time accused each person there of having sinned themselves. Those who wish to judge others should be pure themselves. This verse is sometimes used to excuse sin. The attitude is that we are free from blame because everyone has done things that are wrong. But this verse does not excuse sin; rather, it condemns those who are guilty even though they have never been caught.

Once again, Jesus stooped down and wrote on the ground. Verses 6 and 8 are the only recorded instances of the Lord Jesus writing anything, and whatever He wrote has long been erased from the earth. Those who accused the woman were convicted (v. 9). They had nothing to say. One by one they began to go away. All were guilty, the oldest acting on conviction of conscience on down. Jesus was left standing alone, with the woman nearby. Then, in wonderful grace, the Lord Jesus pointed out to the woman that all her accusers had vanished. Not a single person had dared to condemn her. "Has no one condemned you?" He asked. When the woman said, "No one, Sir," the Lord uttered those wonderful words, "Neither do I condemn you: go and sin no more."

In the first chapter of this gospel, we learned that "grace and truth came by Jesus Christ." Here was an example of that. In the words "Neither do I condemn you," we have an example of grace; the words "Go and sin no more" are words of truth. The Lord did not say, "Go, and sin as little as possible." Jesus Christ is God, and His standard is absolute perfection. He cannot approve of sin in any degree. And so He set before her the perfect standard of God Himself.

> Jesus Christ is God, and His standard is absolute perfection. He cannot approve of sin in any degree.

"I am the light of the world" (8:12-20)

The scene now changed to the treasury of the temple, as we shall learn in verse 20. A multitude was still following Jesus. He turned to them and made one of the many grand statements as to His deity. He said, "I am the light of the world." The world is in the darkness of sin, ignorance, and aimlessness. The Light of the world is Jesus. Apart from Him, there is no deliverance from the blackness of sin, no guidance along the way of life, and no knowledge of the real meaning of life or of the issues of eternity. Jesus promised that anyone following Him would not walk in darkness but would have the light of life. Many people think they can live as Jesus lived without putting their personal faith in Him. But to follow Jesus means to come to Him in repentance, to trust Him as Lord and personal Savior, and then to commit one's whole life to Him, living in light of His authority and wisdom as presented in the Scriptures. Those who do this have guidance in life and a clear, bright hope beyond the grave.

> To follow Jesus means to come to Him in repentance, to trust Him as Lord and personal Savior, and then to commit one's whole life to Him.

The Pharisees, in verse 13, challenged Jesus on a legal point. (It is interesting to note that much of John's gospel reads like a court debate.) They reminded Him He was testifying concerning Himself. A person's own testimony was not considered sufficient because the average person is biased. Verses 14 to 18 record Jesus' response. The Lord recognized that in the Mosaic law, it was necessary to have two or three witnesses. But in His case, His testimony was absolutely true because of who He was. They judged by outward appearances and according to human standards. They looked upon Jesus as a carpenter of Nazareth, never stopping to think how different He was from any other man who had ever lived.

The Lord Jesus said that He judged no one (v. 15). This may mean that He did not judge according to worldly standards as the Pharisees did. Or more probably it meant that His purpose in coming into the world was not to judge people, but to save them. If the Lord *were* to judge, His judgment would be righteous and true. He is God, and everything He did was done in partnership with the Father who sent Him.

Over and over again, the Lord Jesus emphasized to the Pharisees His unity with God the Father. It was this that stirred up in their hearts the bitterest antagonism to Him. The Lord acknowledged that the testimony of two witnesses was required by the Law. Nothing He had said was intended to deny that. So, if they insisted on having two witnesses, it was not difficult to produce them. First, He bore witness of Himself by His sinless life and by what He said. Second, the Father bore witness to Him by public statements from heaven and by the miracles He gave Christ to do. The Lord Jesus fulfilled the prophecies of the Old Testament concerning the Christ, and yet in face of this strong evidence, the Jewish leaders were unwilling to believe.

The Pharisees' next question, contained in verse 19, was no doubt spoken in scorn. Perhaps they looked around the crowd as they said, "Where is Your Father?" His answer was that as they did not recognize who He truly was, they did know His Father either. Of course, they would have denied such ignorance of God, but it was true. If they had received Christ Jesus, they would have known the Father as well. But no man can know God the Father except through Christ. Thus their rejection of Him made it impossible for them to honestly claim that they knew and loved God. The scene of this encounter was the treasury of the temple. Again the Lord was divinely protected and no one could lay a hand on Him to arrest Him or to kill Him. His hour had not yet come. The "hour," of course, refers to the time when He would be crucified at Calvary to die for the sin of the world.

CHAPTER

12

JESUS DEBATES WITH THE PHARISEES
JOHN 8:21-60

"I am going away . . ." (vv. 21-30)

In chapter 8 verse 21, John again records evidence of Christ's perfect knowledge of the future. Christ told His critics He was going to go away—referring not only to His death and burial, but to His resurrection and ascension back to heaven. The Jewish people would continue to seek for the Messiah, not realizing that He had already come. Because they rejected Christ Jesus they would die in their sins and be forever prevented from entering heaven, where Jesus was going. It is a solemn truth! Those who refuse to accept the Lord Jesus have no hope of heaven. How solemn it is to die in one's sins, without God, without Christ, without hope forever.

The Jews did not understand that the Lord spoke of going back to heaven (v. 22). What did He mean by "going away"? Did He mean He would escape from their plot to kill Him by committing suicide? It was strange they should think this. If He were to kill Himself, there would be nothing to prevent them from doing the same and "following" Him. It was just another example of the darkness of unbelief (recall the concepts of darkness and light introduced in the prologue to the gospel). It seems amazing they could be so dull and ignorant of what Jesus was saying! No doubt referring to their foolish reference to suicide, Jesus told them that they were "from beneath," that is, they could not rise above the literal things of time and sense. They had no spiritual understanding. The Lord Jesus, in contrast, was from above. His thoughts, words, and deeds were heavenly in nature. All that they did was of this world; Christ's whole life proclaimed Him to be from a purer land than this world.

Jesus often used repetition for emphasis, so in verse 24 He warned again that they would die in their sins. The word "He" is not found in this verse in the original, though it may be implied. It reads literally, "If you do not believe that I am, you will die in your sins." We see in the words "I am" that Christ is making another claim to deity.

Obviously perplexed, Christ's Jewish audience asked Him pointedly who He was. And His answer? "Just what I have been saying to you from the beginning." From the outset of His earthly ministry, He had told the Jews He was their promised Messiah. Their stubborn hearts refused to bow to the truth. His answer can be taken another way though—that the Lord Jesus in His person embodied exactly what He preached. He did not say one thing and do another; His life agreed with His teaching.

The meaning of verse 26 is not clear. It seems the Lord was saying there were many additional things He could say and judge concerning these unbelieving Jews. He could expose the wicked thoughts and motives of their hearts. However, He was obediently speaking only those things which the Father had given Him to speak. John's editorial comment in verse 27 seems to be for the benefit of his readers: he wanted them to clearly understand that Jesus spoke and did only what God the Father had commissioned Him to say and do.

In verse 28, Jesus again prophesies about the future: that they would "lift up the Son of Man," referring to His death by crucifixion, which John viewed as His exaltation (cf. 3:14; 12:23). After they had done that, they would know indeed He was the Messiah. Dr. Constable comments, "Jesus did not mean His crucifixion would convince all of His critics regarding His true identity, but that exaltation would be the key to many of them believing on Him (cf. 12:32)." Notice carefully Christ's words: "Then you will know that I am He." Here, again, the word "He" is not in the original (it being in italics). Hence He was saying, "Then you will know that I am God." Then they would understand He did nothing from Himself, that is, by His own authority. He came into the world as the dependent One, speaking only those things that the Father had taught Him to speak, and His desire was to please the Father in all things.

Christ's relationship with God the Father was an intimate one. Each of the expressions in verse 29 was a claim to equality with God. Throughout His earthly ministry, the Father was with Him. At no time was Jesus left alone. At all times He did the things that were pleasing to God. These words could only be spoken by a sinless being. No man born of human parents could truthfully utter such words as these—"I always do those things that please Him." We do things that please ourselves or that please our fellow men. Only Christ Jesus was completely taken up with the things that were well-pleasing to God. After saying this, many professed to believe in Him, and no doubt some were genuine in their faith (8:30). Others might have been giving only lip service to Him.

"The truth shall make you free" (vv. 31-36)

Jesus made a distinction in verses 31 and 32 between those who are disciples and those who are "disciples indeed." A disciple is anyone who professes to be a learner, but a "disciple indeed" is one who has definitely committed himself to his or her teacher—in this case, to Christ. True believers in Christ have this characteristic: they continue in "His word," that is they continue in (hold to, live by) His teachings. They do not turn aside from Him. True faith always has the quality of permanence. We are not *saved* by keeping Christ's teachings, but we continue (abide, remain) in His word *because* we are saved.

> We are not *saved* by keeping Christ's teachings, but we *continue* in His word because we are saved.

The promise is now made to every true disciple that he will know the truth, and the truth will make him free. The Jews did not know the truth and were thus in terrible bondage to ignorance, error, sin, law, and superstition. Those who truly know the Lord Jesus are delivered from sin, they walk in the light, and they are led by the Holy Spirit of God. Some of the Jews who were standing by heard the Lord's reference to being made free. They resented it immediately. They boasted of their descent from Abraham and asserted that they had never been enslaved (v. 33). But that was not true: Israel had been in bondage to Egypt, Assyria, Babylon, Persia, Greece, and now Rome! But even more than that, the Jews were in bondage to sin and to Satan, and this is what Jesus was speaking about.

Those who practice sin are the slaves of sin. These Jews pretended to be very religious, but the truth of the matter was that they were dishonest, irreverent, and intending murderers—for even now they were plotting the death of the Christ, the very Son of God.

Jesus next compared the relative positions in a house of a slave and a son. The slave did not have any assurance he would live there forever; the son was at home in the house. Does the word "Son" apply to the Son of God, or does it apply to those who become children of God by faith in Christ? Whichever view is accepted, Jesus was telling these Jews they were not sons, but slaves. There is no question that the word "Son" in verse 36 refers to Christ Himself. Those who are made free by Him are made free indeed. When a person comes to the Savior, he or she is freed from the slavery of sin, legalism, superstition, and demonism.

"You are of your father the devil" (8:37-47)

The Lord now acknowledged that, as far as physical descent was concerned, these Jews *were* Abraham's seed. But it was evident they were not of the spiritual seed of Abraham. They could not be characterized as men of faith, which Abraham was. They sought to kill Jesus because they refused to believe He was the Son of God. They resisted His doctrines and would not yield to Him. The things Jesus taught them were things the Father had commissioned Him to speak. He and His Father were so completely one that the words He spoke were the words of the Father. The Lord Jesus perfectly represented His Father while here on the earth. In contrast, the Jews did those things which they had learned from *their* father. The Lord Jesus did not mean their literal, earthly fathers, but *the devil*.

> The Lord Jesus perfectly represented His Father while here on the earth.

In verse 39 the Jews once again claimed kinship to Abraham and boasted that Abraham was their father. Jesus pointed out that they did not have the characteristics of Abraham's children. Abraham always took his place on the side of truth and righteousness. It was very clear who their father was because they acted just like him. Their father was the devil. The words of the Jews in verse 41 seem to be accusing the Lord of being born of fornication. Most Bible students, however, see in the word "fornication" a reference to idolatry. The Jews were saying they had never committed spiritual adultery. They had always been true to God. He is the only One whom they ever acknowledged as their Father.

In verse 42 the Lord showed the falseness of their claim by reminding them that if they loved God, they would love Him whom God had sent. It is foolish to claim to love God and at the same time to hate the Lord Jesus Christ. Jesus said He came forth from God—that is, He was the eternally begotten Son of God. This relationship of Son to the Father existed from all eternity. He also reminded them that He came forth from God. Obviously, He was proclaiming His pre-existence. He dwelt in heaven with the Father long before He appeared on this earth. But the Father sent Him into the world to be the Savior of the world, and He was obedient to that mission.

There is a difference in verse 43 between "speech" and "word." Christ's *word* referred to the things He taught; His *speech* referred to the words with which He expressed His truths. They could not even understand His speech. When He spoke of bread, they thought of literal bread. When He spoke of water, they thought of literal water. Why could they not understand His speech? It was because they were unwilling to tolerate His teachings and they had no spiritual insight.

Now the Lord Jesus came out openly in verse 44 and told them the devil was their father. As Augustine said, they were children of the devil by imitation. They showed their relationship to the devil by living the way he lived. "The desires of your father you want to do." It is an expression of the intention and desire of their hearts.

The devil was a murderer from the beginning. He brought death to Adam and the whole human race. He was a liar as well. He did not stand in the truth because there is no truth in him. When he told a lie, he was merely expressing his nature. He is a liar and the father of lies. The Jews imitated the devil in these two ways. They were murderers because their intention was to kill the Son of God, and they were liars because they insisted that God was their Father. They pretended to be godly, spiritual men, but in reality they were wicked. Those who give themselves over to lying seem to lose the capacity for discerning the truth. The Lord Jesus had always spoken the truth to these men, yet they would not believe Him. This showed that their real character was wicked.

Only Christ, the sinless Son of God, could truly utter words like these recorded in verse 46. Not one person could convict Him of a single sin. There was no defect in His character. He spoke only words of truth, and yet they would not believe Him. If a man really loves God, he will hear and obey the words of God. The Jews showed by their rejection of Christ's message that they did not really belong to God.

> If a man really loves God, he will hear and obey the words of God.

"Before Abraham was, I am" (vv. 48-59)

In verse 48 we see that once again the Jews resorted to abusive language because they could not answer the Lord in any other way. In calling Him "a Samaritan," they used a term of reproach, implying He was a half-breed, not a pure Jew. They also accused Him of being demon-possessed. By this they no doubt meant He was insane. To them, only a man out of his mind would make the claims Jesus had been making. Notice in verse 49 the even-tempered way that Jesus answered His enemies. His words were not those of one who had a devil but of One who sought to honor God the Father. They should have known that at no time did He seek His own glory. All He did was calculated to bring glory to His Father (v. 50). Then the Lord Jesus added the words, "There is One who seeks and judges," referring to God. God the Father would seek glory for His beloved Son and would judge all of those who failed to give Him this glory.

> Those who believe in the Lord are delivered from eternal death and will never suffer the pangs of hell.

In verse 51 we have one of those majestic sayings of the Lord Jesus, words that could only be uttered by One who was God Himself. The words are introduced by the familiar expression, "Most assuredly, I say to you . . ." The Lord Jesus promised that if a man kept His saying, that man would never see death. This cannot refer to physical death because many believers in the Lord Jesus die each day. The reference is to spiritual death. The Lord was saying that those who believe in Him are delivered from eternal death and will never suffer the pangs of hell.

The Jews were more convinced than ever that Jesus was mad—after all, Abraham and the prophets were all dead, yet He had said that if a man kept His sayings he would not see death! How could these statements be reconciled? They realized the Lord was claiming to be greater than Abraham and the prophets. Abraham never delivered anyone from death, and could not deliver himself from death. Neither could the prophets. Yet here was One who claimed to be able to deliver His fellow men from death. He must consider Himself greater than the patriarchs.

The Jews thought Jesus was seeking to attract attention to Himself (v. 54). He denied this. It was God the Father who was honoring Him, the very God whom they professed to love and serve. The Jews did not even know God. Yet here they were speaking with One who knew the Father intimately, One who was equal with Him! They wanted Jesus to deny His equality with the Father, but He said if He did this, He would be a liar. He knew God the Father and obeyed His words.

> **Jesus claimed to be the fulfillment of all the prophecies in the Old Testament concerning the Messiah.**

Since the Jews insisted on bringing Abraham into the argument, Jesus reminded them in verse 56 that Abraham had looked forward to the day of the Messiah, and that he had actually seen it by faith and was glad. Abraham's faith rested in the coming of Jesus Christ. Thus Jesus claimed to be the fulfillment of all the prophecies in the Old Testament concerning the Messiah.

The next verse (v. 57) testifies again to the Jews' inability to understand divine truth. Jesus had said, "Abraham rejoiced *to see My day* . . ." but they replied as though He had implied *He had seen Abraham*. There is a great difference here. The Lord was really claiming for Himself a position greater than Abraham. He was the Object of Abraham's thoughts and hopes. Abraham looked forward by faith to Christ's day. The Jews could not understand this. They reasoned that Jesus was not yet fifty years old. (Actually, He was only about thirty-three years old at this time.) So, how could He have seen Abraham?

In verse 58, the Lord made another clear claim to deity. He did not say, "Before Abraham was, I was." That might simply mean He came into existence before Abraham. Rather, He used the Name of God, I AM. The Lord had dwelt with God the Father from all eternity. There was never a time when He came into being, or when He did not exist. Therefore, He said, "Before Abraham was, I AM." At once the wicked Jews attempted to put Jesus to death, but in a miraculous way He moved out of their midst and left the temple. The Jews understood exactly what Jesus meant: He was claiming to be Jehovah. It was for this reason they sought to stone Him, because to them this was blasphemy. They were unwilling to accept the fact that the Messiah was in their midst. They refused to allow Him to reign over them.

THE GOSPEL OF

JOHN

Part 1
Chapters 1–8

Exam Booklet
AK '17 (2 Units) JOHN1

Student Name (please print)

Address

City, State, Zip

Course Grade: _____

Instructor

Exam developed by Emmaus Correspondence School, founded in 1942.

A NOTE ON THE EXAMS

The exams are designed to check your knowledge of the course material and the Scriptures. After you have studied a chapter, review the exam questions for that lesson. If you have difficulty in answering the questions, re-read the material. If questions contain a Scripture reference, you may use your Bible to help you answer them. If your instructor has provided a Single Page Answer Sheet, record your answer on that sheet. This exam contains the following types of questions:

MULTIPLE CHOICE

You will be asked to write in the letter of the correct answer at the space on the right. Here is an example:

The color of grass is

| A. blue. | C. yellow. |
| B. green. | D. orange. |

B

WHAT DO YOU SAY?

Questions headed this way are designed to help you express your ideas and feelings. You may freely state your own opinions in answer to such questions.

RETURNING THE EXAM

See the last page of this exam section for instructions on returning your exam for grading.

> DO NOT PHOTOCOPY THESE EXAM PAGES

First Edition 2017 (AK '17), 2 UNITS
ISBN 978-1-59387-148-2
Code: JOHN1
Copyright © 2017 ECS Ministries

All rights reserved. No part of this publication may be reproduced or transmitted in any form or by any means, electronic or mechanical.

Printed in the United States of America

CHAPTER 1 EXAM

Jesus Christ Is God Incarnate

EXAM GRADE _____

Before starting this exam, write your name and address on the front of this Exam Booklet.

Read each question carefully and write the letter of the correct answer in the blank space on the right. Use the separate answer sheet if provided.

1. The apostle John expressed his purpose for writing this book in
   A. John 1:1.   C. John 20:31.
   B. John 3:16. D. John 10:30.   _____

2. The miracles performed by Jesus that John included in his gospel point to the fact that
   A. Jesus is God.   C. Jesus is compassionate.
   B. Jesus is powerful.   D. Jesus is super-human.   _____

3. The _____ of Jesus' earthly ministry is gained from this gospel.
   A. extent   C. reason
   B. chronology   D. political context   _____

4. What is conveyed by John's use of the term "the Word" in referring to Jesus?
   A. God has fully expressed Himself to mankind in Jesus Christ.
   B. Jesus spoke many words during His time on earth.
   C. The words that Jesus spoke only came from the Old Testament Scriptures.
   D. The words that Jesus spoke needed to be interpreted in order to be understood.   _____

5. The first 5 verses of chapter 1 describe the Word as
   A. Creator.   C. God.
   B. Life.   D. all the above   _____

6. The mission of John the Baptist was to
   A. restore the power of the priesthood.
   B. promote civil disobedience against the Roman government.
   C. announce the coming of Christ.
   D. write the New Testament. _____

7. As "the true Light,"
   A. Jesus gave each man some inward knowledge of God.
   B. Jesus revealed what man is really like.
   C. Jesus made sure every Jew was "enlightened" about Him at some time or other.
   D. Jesus had a soft glow about His person. _____

8. When the world's Creator came to live in this world,
   A. most people rejected Him.
   B. everyone rejected Him.
   C. the Jews gladly received Him.
   D. the Gentiles gladly received Him. _____

9. We can become children of God by
   A. doing good works.
   B. joining a church.
   C. making sure our righteousness exceeds our wrongdoing.
   D. receiving Jesus Christ, believing in Him. _____

10. When "the Word became flesh,"
    A. He made appearances to certain people.
    B. He came to live among human beings.
    C. He ceased to be God.
    D. He lived in a commune. _____

WHAT DO YOU SAY?

What is your personal response to the multi-faceted description of Jesus Christ given in these verses?

_____

_____

_____

_____

CHAPTER 2 EXAM

John the Baptist Fulfills His Mission

EXAM GRADE

Write the letter of the correct answer in the blank space on the right. Use the separate answer sheet if provided.

1. John the Baptist declared himself to be
   A. the predicted Voice.
   B. the predicted Prophet.
   C. Elijah.
   D. the Christ.

2. John's message was
   A. "Come, follow me."
   B. "Make straight the way of the Lord."
   C. "I have greater authority than the priests."
   D. "My cousin is the one you are waiting for."

3. John's baptism was
   A. a means of having sins forgiven.
   B. how the Jews declared they had become John's disciples.
   C. a new way for Gentiles to convert to Judaism.
   D. an outward symbol of an inward change of heart.

4. Why did John call Jesus the Lamb of God?
   A. His temperament resembled a lamb's—calm, gentle.
   B. He would bear away the sin of the world.
   C. The lamb's white skin/coat symbolized His purity.
   D. Like a lamb, He was helpless to control what would happen to Him.

5. It was at the time of Jesus' _____ that John first realized Jesus was the Messiah.
   A. first miracle
   B. baptism
   C. calling of His disciples
   D. entry into Jerusalem

6. When John baptized Jesus in the Jordan,
   A. everyone cheered.
   B. the Pharisees complained to John.
   C. the Holy Spirit descended and rested on Jesus.
   D. the people watching were confused.

7. The Hebrew term for "teacher" is
   A. Messiah.
   B. Rabbi.
   C. Yahweh.
   D. Christ.

8. Andrew's first reaction upon meeting Jesus was to
   A. sell his fishing business and follow Him.
   B. go home and tell his brother Simon that he had found the Messiah.
   C. introduce Nathanael to Christ.
   D. be baptized in the River Jordan.

9. The next day, Jesus went to Galilee and invited _____ to follow Him.
   A. Philip
   B. Levi
   C. Judas
   D. James

10. When Nathanael met Jesus, Jesus demonstrated His deity and messiahship by
    A. revealing Nathanael's character and where he had been sitting.
    B. healing Nathanael's long-standing illness.
    C. showing Nathanael a vision of angels and predicting the future.
    D. talking about Nathanael's family heritage and comparing it to Philip's.

What Do You Say?

What is one lesson you take away from this portion about telling people about Christ?

_____

_____

_____

_____

CHAPTER 3 EXAM

Jesus Begins His Public Ministry

EXAM GRADE

Write the letter of the correct answer in the blank space on the right. Use the separate answer sheet if provided.

1. Jesus and His disciples
   A. retreated to a private place in Galilee.
   B. went about preaching in Capernaum.
   C. were invited to a wedding in Cana.
   D. sought to find other disciples in Galilee. _____

2. Wine is often a picture of _____ in Scripture.
   A. joy   C. contentment
   B. immorality   D. prosperity _____

3. In dealing with the shortage of wine issue, Jesus conveyed to His mother that
   A. in His divine mission, He was not subject to instructions from her.
   B. He was irritated by her interrupting His enjoyment of the festivities.
   C. He was not able to do anything to remedy to the situation.
   D. He was not interested in solving other peoples' problems. _____

4. Mary's last recorded words in Scripture are
   A. "They have no wine."
   B. "I will pray for you."
   C. "He is risen!"
   D. "Whatever He says to you, do it." _____

5. When Jesus turned water into wine, it was
   A. a sin, because He should not have been encouraging the people to drink wine.
   B. an instantaneous miracle.
   C. the third miracle He had performed publicly.
   D. an effort to draw a following. _____

6. As used in the gospel of John, a sign is
   A. a symbol of something that had happened.
   B. a miracle "pointing" to the fact that Jesus was Israel's promised Messiah.
   C. a notice to give directions to a certain place.
   D. an illustration of an Old Testament event. _____

7. The Lord cleansed the temple at Passover time
   A. at the beginning and in the middle of His public ministry.
   B. only at the end of His public ministry.
   C. every time He went there.
   D. at the beginning and the end of His public ministry. _____

8. The Passover was an annual feast commemorating
   A. the bringing in of the harvest.
   B. the Israelites' deliverance from slavery in Egypt.
   C. the building of the temple.
   D. Israel's return from captivity in Babylon. _____

9. In answering the Jews' demand for a miracle to prove His authority, Jesus
   A. spoke of His miraculous birth.
   B. predicted His own death and resurrection.
   C. reminded them of His turning water into wine.
   D. healed one of them who was diseased. _____

10. The statement that Jesus "knew all men" meant
    A. He must have studied psychology.
    B. He was an astute observer of human nature.
    C. He knew what was in the heart of man.
    D. He had great memory skills. _____

What Do You Say?

Reflecting back on John 1:14, which verses in this section demonstrate that Jesus was (a) "full of grace" and (b) "full of truth"?

_____
_____
_____
_____

CHAPTER 4 EXAM

JESUS AND JOHN THE BAPTIST REVEAL THE WAY INTO THE KINGDOM

EXAM GRADE

Write the letter of the correct answer in the blank space on the right. Use the separate answer sheet if provided.

1. Nicodemus was
   A. a Roman citizen.
   B. a fisherman in Galilee.
   C. a teacher among the Jews.
   D. a tax collector.

2. To be fit to be to a citizen of God's kingdom, a person must
   A. be a Jew.
   B. be prepared to die for his faith.
   C. be both righteous and willing to submit to the King.
   D. be baptized.

3. Jesus told Nicodemus he must be born of water and the Spirit. What did He most likely mean by this?
   A. Spiritual birth is produced by the Holy Spirit of God.
   B. Baptism by water is necessary for the new birth.
   C. Water refers to the role Scripture has in our salvation.
   D. Only human beings (those "born of water"), not angels, can be born spiritually.

4. To illustrate the nature of the new birth, Jesus compared it to
   A. waves on the sea.   C. water.
   B. the wind.   D. nature in spring time.

5. In the OT event Jesus referenced, the bronze snake was
   A. placed on the bite of each ailing Israelite to cure them.
   B. worshiped by the whole nation, then sacrificed to.
   C. buried in the sand and dug up again after 3 days.
   D. lifted high on a pole. Those who looked at it, as instructed, were cured.

6. John 3:16 teaches that
   A. all the world will be saved, because God loves everybody.
   B. eternal life is the free gift of God to all who believe in His Son.
   C. believing in Jesus just means believing He existed.
   D. God must love people more than His Son to have given Him up like that.

7. According to verse 18, a person remains under condemnation for his sinful state if he
   A. does not believe in Jesus Christ.
   B. has committed sexual offences of any sort.
   C. commits the unpardonable sin.
   D. makes no effort to keep the 10 commandments.

8. To be willing to expose one's own sinfulness to the light of Christ's purity
   A. is a mark of genuine conversion.
   B. is damaging to one's self esteem.
   C. is required, along with confessing to a priest, in order to be saved.
   D. is not expected of children who want to be saved.

9. One way John demonstrated his humility was in describing himself as
   A. the door-keeper of heaven.
   B. a bond-slave of the Lord.
   C. the servant of Christ.
   D. the friend of the Bridegroom.

10. "Our eternal destiny
    A. is the focus of these final verses of the chapter."
    B. depends on what we do with the Son of God."
    C. is not dependent on our good works but on our love for Christ."
    D. is set before we are even born."

WHAT DO YOU SAY?
How has the teaching on this section furthered your understanding of salvation?

_____
_____
_____
_____

CHAPTER 5 EXAM

Jesus Reveals Himself
to the Samaritans

EXAM GRADE

Write the letter of the correct answer in the blank space on the right.
Use the separate answer sheet if provided.

1. Jesus had to go through Samaria because
   A. that was the most direct route to Galilee, and He was in a hurry.
   B. the alternate route through Perea was inaccessible at that time of year.
   C. He was tired and hoped to find accommodations in Sychar.
   D. there were many spiritually needy souls there.

2. The woman at the well was amazed that Jesus would speak to her because
   A. He was a Jew and she was a Samaritan.
   B. it was so early in the morning.
   C. few people could speak Aramaic, which was her native tongue.
   D. there were so many people watching.

3. When Jesus offered the woman _____, she immediately wanted it.
   A. food
   B. a seat beside Him
   C. living water
   D. shade from the sun

4. Why did Jesus tell the woman to go call her husband?
   A. To find out if she was married
   B. He preferred talking to men.
   C. To convict her of her sin
   D. To embarrass her

5. In His conversation with the woman, Jesus revealed that
   A. God has stipulated only one place to worship Him: in Jerusalem.
   B. God seeks and desires genuine worship from His people.
   C. the Jews were worshiping God correctly, and the Samaritans, incorrectly.
   D. worshiping God from the heart is all that matters; what we say or do is secondary.

6. Jesus assured the woman that He was
   A. a reliable Jewish teacher.
   B. the forerunner of the Messiah.
   C. the Messiah the Samaritans had been waiting for.
   D. a God-appointed mediator trying to reconcile Jews and Gentiles.

7. The Samaritan woman's next step upon leaving the well was to
   A. tell her fellow townspeople that she had found the Christ.
   B. get very upset at what Jesus had said to her.
   C. curse the Jews for their scorn and exclusiveness.
   D. go back for the water-pot she had forgotten.

8. Jesus described fulfilling the mission God had given Him as
   A. distasteful.   C. character-building.
   B. a joy.   D. food.

9. When Jesus told the disciples that the fields were ready for harvest, He was
   A. instructing them to harvest the wheat fields.
   B. speaking of a *spiritual* harvest.
   C. encouraging them to become farmers.
   D. telling them where to get food.

10. As a result of spending time with Jesus, the Samaritans came to know that
    A. He was a good man, empowered by God.
    B. He was the Christ, the Savior of the world.
    C. He was willing to help them with their harvest.
    D. they needed to go to Jerusalem to worship God.

THE GOSPEL OF JOHN – PART 1　　　　　　　　　　　　　　　　AK '17

WHAT DO YOU SAY?

From this section give at least one current-day application from Christ's concern for the lost.

_____

_____

_____

_____

CHAPTER 6 EXAM

JESUS MINISTERS TO INDIVIDUALS IN GALILEE AND JERUSALEM

EXAM GRADE

Write the letter of the correct answer in the blank space on the right. Use the separate answer sheet if provided.

1. When Jesus returned to Galilee He received a favorable reception because
   A. He was a loyal home-town boy.
   B. people wanted to see many miracles in their area.
   C. He had promised to free them from Roman domination.
   D. people had seen the things He had done in Jerusalem. _____

2. A nobleman came from Capernaum, _____ miles away, to seek healing for his dying son.
   A. 5   C. 13
   B. 7   D. 25   _____

3. When Jesus said to the nobleman, "Your son lives," the man's response was
   A. to beg Jesus to come home with him.
   B. to believe what Jesus said and start for home.
   C. to be very disappointed in Jesus' lack of interest.
   D. to think Jesus was just brushing him off. _____

4. By going to Jerusalem for the feast, Jesus
   A. was able to increase His following.
   B. was able to visit with His relatives.
   C. was obedient to the laws God had made for the Jewish people.
   D. was able to implement His plan for intimidating the Pharisees. _____

5. Jesus approached a man lying beside the pool of Bethesda. What did He say to him?
   A. "Do you want to be made well?"
   B. "How long have you been here?"
   C. "I can help you into the pool."
   D. "The angel won't come today." _____

6. Because Jesus healed the man _____, the Jews challenged him for carrying his bed.
   A. on the Sabbath
   B. in public
   C. without their permission
   D. even though he was a sinner

7. In what realm did the course author describe God as working constantly?
   A. In sustaining the seasons
   B. In speaking to mankind through prophets
   C. In working out His plan to provide man with redemption from sin
   D. In waging a spiritual war with Satan

8. The Jews were determined to kill Jesus because
   A. He tried to take their place as leaders of Israel.
   B. He claimed to be equal with God.
   C. He made friends with the Romans.
   D. He taught things contrary to the Mosaic law.

9. The "greater works" that Christ said He would do to demonstrate His equality with God included
   A. miraculous healings and authoritative teaching.
   B. imparting life and passing judgment.
   C. powerful preaching and effective praying.
   D. controlling both nature and people.

10. According to verse 23, why has God given authority to His Son?
    A. So people will be afraid of the Son
    B. So people will listen to the Son
    C. So people will honor the Son as they do the Father
    D. So people will stop persecuting the Son

What Do You Say?

Identify at least 3 divine characteristics of Christ from this lesson's passage. What should our response be?

_____

_____

_____

_____

THE GOSPEL OF JOHN – PART 1   AK '17

CHAPTER 7 EXAM

JESUS DEFENDS HIS GOD-GIVEN AUTHORITY

EXAM GRADE

Write the letter of the correct answer in the blank space on the right. Use the separate answer sheet if provided.

1. If a person believes what God says about His Son, he/she
   A. has everlasting life from the point of believing in Christ.
   B. will have everlasting life after he/she dies.
   C. will have a prosperous life.
   D. has all he/she needs for a good life.

2. "To hear the word of Jesus" means
   A. to receive it.   C. to obey it.
   B. to believe it.   D. all the above

3. The course author points out that Jesus' ability to give life to those who believe in Him affirms
   A. His power.   C. His wisdom.
   B. His grace.   D. His deity.

4. Christ's statement, "I can of Myself do nothing," implies that
   A. It was morally impossible for Him to not fulfill the will of His Father.
   B. He was physically incapable of resisting the will of His Father.
   C. as a man, He gave up any right to do what He wanted.
   D. He really could not have been fully God as well as man.

5. The five witnesses that Jesus cited to authenticate His deity were
   A. a. His Father, the Spirit, His mother, the Scriptures, and John the Baptist.
   B. His Father, His miracles, John the Baptist, Moses, and His disciples.
   C. His Father, Moses, His mother, John the Baptist, and His disciples.
   D. His Father, John the Baptist, His miraculous signs, the Scriptures, and Moses.

E 17

THE GOSPEL OF JOHN – PART 1   AK '17

6. Jesus described John the Baptist as
   A. a holy man.
   B. a cousin of His.
   C. a burning and shining lamp.
   D. His forerunner.

7. "[Jesus'] miracles were unique in _____, _____, and _____."
   A. character, scope, and number
   B. character, variety, and volume
   C. location, subjects, and purpose
   D. purpose, magnitude, and variety

8. The Lord Jesus referred the Jews back to the OT Scriptures, because in them they would
   A. find salvation even if they rejected Him.
   B. find plenty of reasons for arguing with Him.
   C. discover that they revealed Him.
   D. find hidden all the truths unfolded in the NT.

9. The course author comments that the real reason many people do not take Jesus as their Savior is that
   A. they do not understand the gospel.
   B. they think that He's not able to truly save them.
   C. they are afraid of the repercussions of doing so.
   D. they are not willing to give up their sins.

10. Jesus stated that if the Jews truly believed _____, they would have believed Him also.
    A. Abraham
    B. Moses
    C. David
    D. Isaiah

WHAT DO YOU SAY?

Rewrite John 5:24-25 in your own words.

_____
_____
_____
_____

CHAPTER 8 EXAM

JESUS FEEDS 5000+ AND TEACHES ON THE BREAD FROM HEAVEN

EXAM GRADE

Write the letter of the correct answer in the blank space on the right. Use the separate answer sheet if provided.

1. The Passover John mentions in 6:4 was the one
   A. when Jesus was a child.
   B. just after Jesus' baptism.
   C. a year before Jesus' death.
   D. when Jesus was crucified.

2. The fact that _____ conveys that this narrative is very significant.
   A. this sign is recorded each of the four gospels
   B. Jesus spoke directly to the people
   C. the disciples had jobs to do
   D. Jesus spent time in prayer

3. Whenever Jesus asked a question it was
   A. to discover information He didn't know about.
   B. to introduce a new subject.
   C. with the intent of using it as a teaching tool.
   D. to help people feel at ease with Him.

4. In answer to the question of how they would feed 5000+ people, Andrew stated
   A. there was a town nearby where they could buy food.
   B. there was a boy who had five barley loaves and two small fish.
   C. it was impossible to find that much food.
   D. they should teach them and then send them home.

5. How did Jesus calm the disciples during a storm on the Sea of Galilee?
   A. He scolded them for not believing.
   B. He helped them row to the shore.
   C. He sang songs of comfort from the Psalms.
   D. He came to them and declared who He was.

6. When Jesus got into the boat with the disciples,
   A. they were immediately at their destination.
   B. He helped them row to the shore.
   C. He told them they should not have been afraid.
   D. they questioned Him about His power. _____

7. The goal of Jesus' miracles was primarily
   A. to make people happy and healthy.
   B. that people would learn lessons of spiritual truth.
   C. that He would draw more followers.
   D. that He would become a popular leader. _____

8. Jesus used the occasion to compare the value of
   A. listening to Him with listening to the rabbis.
   B. physical food with spiritual food.
   C. following Him with farming their fields.
   D. submitting to the Romans with following the Pharisees. _____

9. In reply to the people's question about what work they should do, Jesus replied,
   A. "You must give more to the poor."
   B. "You must be faithful in public worship."
   C. "You must do penance for your sins."
   D. "You must believe in Him whom [God] sent." _____

10. Why did the Jews talk about the manna God gave their ancestors in the wilderness?
    A. They were reminding Jesus of their national history.
    B. They were implying that they were more spiritually aware than Jesus was.
    C. They were implying that Jesus was not as great as Moses.
    D. They were showing off their knowledge to the crowd. _____

What Do You Say?

The feeding of the 5000 is very well-known. What do you enjoy about it?

_____

_____

_____

_____

CHAPTER 9 EXAM

Jesus Is the Bread of Life

EXAM GRADE

Write the letter of the correct answer in the blank space on the right.
Use the separate answer sheet if provided.

1. In John 6:35, Jesus stated that He is
   A. the resurrection and the life.
   B. the door.
   C. the bread of life.
   D. the light of the world.

2. All those chosen by God will
   A. come to Jesus.
   B. automatically be saved.
   C. struggle to find Him.
   D. find themselves forced to submit to His will.

3. Verse 37 teaches two vital truths. The first is,
   A. everyone will eventually be saved.
   B. all those the Father has given to the Son will be saved.
   C. Jesus will raise everyone from the dead.
   D. the Father has set His seal of approval on Jesus.

4. The second important truth stated in verse 37 is,
   A. there are several ways to be saved.
   B. Jesus came down from heaven to be the Father's representative.
   C. Jesus is God.
   D. People must come to Christ in faith to be saved.

5. The Jews believed that Jesus was
   A. the son of Mary and Joseph, an ordinary man.
   B. the Son of God, just as He taught.
   C. superior to Moses.
   D. the bread which had come down from heaven.

6. The Father draws people by
   A. the difficulties of life they go through, realizing they need Him.
   B. the guilt of an unrighteous life, attracted by His holiness.
   C. the teaching of Scripture.
   D. the witness of other believers.

7. In contrast to manna, which was for this life only, Jesus referred to Himself as
   A. the bread which had come down from heaven, of which one may eat and not die.
   B. the source of eternal life for all the Jews under the sound of His voice there and then.
   C. the bread of heaven, earth, and sky, giving life to all mortals and angelic beings.
   D. the breath of God, by which He imparted life to all who would have faith in Him.

8. To eat of Jesus' flesh means
   A. to believe in Him, to appropriate Him into one's life.
   B. to partake of the communion elements.
   C. to read about Him in the Bible.
   D. to pray in His name.

9. Jesus' statement, "The bread that I shall give is My flesh, which I shall give for the life of the world," was a reference to
   A. the next time He would feed a multitude.
   B. an animal sacrifice He would make at the temple in Jerusalem.
   C. His coming sacrificial death on the cross.
   D. His baiting the Pharisees.

10. Jesus promised that those who put their trust in Him would
    A. never die.
    B. have authority in the world to come.
    C. be raised up at the last day.
    D. never need to eat real bread again to stay alive.

WHAT DO YOU SAY?
How has Jesus, the Bread of Life, "satisfied" you?

_____

_____

_____

_____

CHAPTER 10 EXAM

Jesus' Teaching Creates Controversy

EXAM GRADE

Write the letter of the correct answer in the blank space on the right. Use the separate answer sheet if provided.

1. The term "disciples" is applied to
   A. those who followed Jesus and professed to accept His teachings.
   B. only the Twelve whom Jesus selected to be with Him.
   C. those who listened to Jesus, even though they didn't believe what He said.
   D. only those who hoped He would deliver them from the Romans.

2. When some of Jesus' followers said, "This is a hard saying," they meant that
   A. they couldn't understand what He said.
   B. it was different from what they were used to hearing.
   C. His teaching wasn't worth listening to and they were leaving.
   D. His teaching offended them.

3. It is only through _____ that we receive eternal life.
   A. eating Christ's flesh
   B. the Spirit of God and eating Christ's flesh
   C. listening to Christ's teaching
   D. the Spirit of God

4. When Jesus asked the Twelve if they would leave Him as well, Peter answered (in John 6:68-69),
   A. "Lord, we are very confused."
   B. "Lord, to whom shall we go?"
   C. "Lord, some of us might leave."
   D. "Lord, we have to think about it."

The Gospel of John – Part 1

5. Jesus stayed in Galilee because
   A. He wanted to preach to all who would listen there.
   B. life was easier there.
   C. the Jewish leaders in Judea were trying to kill Him.
   D. His family was there.

6. The Feast of Tabernacles celebrated the time when
   A. the tabernacle was first built.
   B. the Israelites lived in tents when they came out of Egypt.
   C. the Israelites went camping with their families.
   D. the fields were planted with seed.

7. Jesus told His brothers that He would not go to Judea just yet for the feast because
   A. He was sick and not able to travel.
   B. His time was not yet fully come.
   C. He still had a lot to do in Galilee.
   D. He was afraid of the Jews who planned to kill Him.

8. Although many of the people probably recognized Jesus to be the Christ, they did not say so openly because
   A. they feared the Jewish leaders.
   B. He had forbidden them to do so.
   C. they expected Him to make a public announcement soon.
   D. they were afraid of a war with Rome.

9. Jesus' teaching was marked by the fact that
   A. He was a gifted communicator.
   B. He had been well-taught as a child.
   C. He sought only to glorify the Father by what He said.
   D. He knew how to create a response from His audience.

10. John records that the Jews were trying to kill Jesus because
    A. He was threatening their life-style.
    B. He had healed a lame man on the Sabbath.
    C. He taught with authority.
    D. He was gathering a following.

WHAT DO YOU SAY?
The Jews were so quick to resist and even attack Christ's teachings. What practical lesson does this have for us?

_____

_____

_____

CHAPTER 11 EXAM

JESUS IS THE LIGHT OF THE WORLD

EXAM GRADE

Write the letter of the correct answer in the blank space on the right. Use the separate answer sheet if provided.

1. The people in Jerusalem "could not understand
   A. what Jesus was teaching them."
   B. why Jesus was being allowed to speak so openly and fearlessly."
   C. why the Jewish leaders hadn't arrested Jesus by now."
   D. why Jesus hadn't become their king by now." _____

2. Many people believed Jesus was the Christ because of
   A. His miracles.
   B. His teaching.
   C. His many kindnesses.
   D. how He debated so well with the Jewish leaders. _____

3. On the last day of the feast, Jesus urged the people to come to Him for
   A. political liberation.
   B. relief from burdens of the Law.
   C. spiritual satisfaction.
   D. healing. _____

4. The living water the Lord Jesus promised to those who believe on Him is
   A. fresh insight into the Scriptures.
   B. eternal life.
   C. the Holy Spirit.
   D. water baptism. _____

5. People thought Jesus had been born in
   A. Jerusalem.   C. Nazareth.
   B. Bethlehem.   D. Capernaum. _____

6. Why were Jesus' enemies unable to arrest Him when they tried to?
   A. He was physically stronger than them and managed to elude them.
   B. His disciples guarded Him well.
   C. He kept Himself hidden.
   D. His time to die had not yet come. _____

7. The scribes and Pharisees tried to trap Jesus by
   A. bringing Him to the attention of the Roman government.
   B. arresting several of His disciples.
   C. bringing before Him a woman caught in adultery to see how He would react.
   D. accusing Him of adultery. _____

8. What Jesus said in 8:7, "He who is without sin among you . . ."
   A. excuses sin if someone has not been caught.
   B. condemns those who are guilty even if they have not been caught.
   C. implies that He had no right to judge others.
   D. upheld the Jewish leaders' responsibility to pass judgment. _____

9. To follow Jesus means to
   A. try to live a good life as He did.
   B. trust Him as Lord and Savior and live in the light of His revealed word.
   C. join a church and follow their rules.
   D. die for one's beliefs. _____

10. The fact that the Pharisees would ask Jesus where His Father was proved
    A. they were genuinely interested in authenticating His claim to deity.
    B. they were very clever at trying to trap people.
    C. they did not know or love His Father.
    D. they realized He was speaking the truth after all. _____

What Do You Say?

Identify some evidences of Christ's character here that make Him worthy of our worship.

_____

_____

_____

_____

CHAPTER 12 EXAM

JESUS DEBATES WITH THE PHARISEES

EXAM GRADE

Write the letter of the correct answer in the blank space on the right.
Use the separate answer sheet if provided.

1. Jesus showed His perfect knowledge of the future when He said to His critics,
   A. "You are trying to kill me."
   B. "My disciples will all desert Me."
   C. "I am going away. . . . Where I go you cannot come."
   D. "You are going to crucify Me." _____

2. The phrase "lift up the Son of Man"
   A. refers to Christ's coming execution by crucifixion.
   B. appears for the first time here in John's gospel.
   C. means there is coming a time when Jesus will be lifted up in praise and honor.
   D. is a prediction of Christ's ascension back to heaven. _____

3. The sign of a true disciple of Jesus is that he or she
   A. leads others to believe in Him.
   B. is active in local church life.
   C. is a real student of the Bible.
   D. continues in what Christ has taught. _____

4. The freedom Jesus was talking about in verse 36 was freedom from
   A. slavery to sin.
   B. Roman rule.
   C. bondage to the Law.
   D. keeping the extra rules the Pharisees set. _____

5. It was evident that these Jews were not the spiritual seed of Abraham because
   A. they denied Abraham as their father.
   B. they were trying to kill Jesus.
   C. they refused to obey the 10 commandments.
   D. they were cohorts of the Romans. _____

6. Jesus stated that _____ was their father.
   A. God
   B. the world
   C. the devil
   D. Cain

7. How did they demonstrate who their father was?
   A. By praising and magnifying him
   B. By teaching about him
   C. By doing the things he does
   D. By recording his words

8. In this chapter, the Jews accused Jesus of
   A. being a friend of tax collectors and sinners.
   B. being Samaritan and having a demon.
   C. being in league with Rome.
   D. being a rebel.

9. "_____ rejoiced to see My day, and he saw it and was glad."
   A. Abraham
   B. Moses
   C. David
   D. Isaiah

10. The Jews tried to stone Jesus when He said,
    A. "I am equal to the Father."
    B. "I am your Messiah."
    C. "Watch and see how I will deliver you."
    D. "Before Abraham was, I AM."

What Do You Say?

If you are a disciple of the Lord Jesus Christ, how has your commitment to follow Him deepened through your study of John's gospel so far? If you are not, what is keeping you from believing in Him?

_____
_____
_____
_____

To send in exam for grading, carefully
tear out exam pages along perforation.

RETURNING THE EXAM BOOKLET FOR GRADING

- ✓ After completing all the exams, check them carefully.
- ✓ <u>Carefully</u> tear out the exam pages along the perforation provided near the book spine.
- ✓ Make sure you have followed all directions.
- ✓ Be sure you have written your correct name and address on all material you will send to the School.
- ✓ Return all the exams at one time instead of separating and mailing each individual exam.
- ✓ Return only the exam section, not the entire course book. If you have used the Single Page Answer Sheet, return only that sheet.
- ✓ Address the envelope correctly.
- ✓ Put the correct postage on the envelope.
- ✓ If you are studying this course through an Associate Instructor or associated ministry or organization, send the exams to the individual or organization from which you obtained the course. Otherwise, send them to the address below.

Emmaus Correspondence School
(A Division of ECS Ministries)
PO Box 1028
Dubuque, Iowa 52004-1028
phone: (563) 585-2070
email: orders@emmauscourses.org
website: www.emmauscourses.org